MANUS-AI
HANDBOOK

The First General Intelligence Agent
Redefining Automation and Innovation

How Autonomous Systems Are
Transforming Work, Disrupting Tech Giants,
and Reshaping the Global Economy

Anthony M. Whitmore

Disclaimer:

The advice and strategies contained herein may only be suitable for some situations. This work is sold with the understanding that the author and publisher are not engaged in rendering professional services. If professional assistance is required, the services of a competent professional should be sought. The author and publisher specifically disclaim any liability incurred from the use or application of the contents of this book.

Table of Contents

Introduction

The Age of AI Agents

The Moment That Changed Everything

On March 6, 2025, an AI system quietly entered the world. It wasn't a chatbot or a search engine upgrade. It didn't just respond to prompts—it acted.

This was Manus AI, the first general intelligence agent, capable of planning, executing, and completing tasks without human guidance. Within hours, those who tested it realized something extraordinary: AI was no longer just a tool—it was a worker.

Unlike ChatGPT, which relied on human interaction, Manus AI could research topics, write and deploy code, analyze financial markets, and even automate entire workflows—all independently. It wasn't an assistant; it was an autonomous intelligence.

And the world took notice.

A Global Frenzy

The launch was invitation-only, but demand exploded overnight. Access codes, initially free, were resold on underground markets for up to $144,000. Tech leaders, AI researchers, and business executives scrambled to understand what they were witnessing:

- Was this the first step toward Artificial General Intelligence (AGI)?
- Had China, through Monica AI, just outpaced OpenAI and Google in the AI race?
- Would AI agents like Manus replace human jobs at scale?

In China, media outlets hailed Manus AI as a "Sputnik moment"—a technological leap that could shift global power. Meanwhile, Silicon Valley insiders debated whether OpenAI's upcoming AI agents were already obsolete.

What made Manus AI so disruptive wasn't just what it could do, but what it represented:

For the first time, AI didn't need humans to function.

Why This Book Matters

We are no longer asking if AI will reshape the world.

It already has.

This book will serve as your comprehensive guide to the rise of autonomous AI agents, breaking down:

- How Manus AI works – its multi-agent system and autonomous capabilities.
- The industries AI agents are transforming – from research to software development.
- The economic and societal impact – how AI could replace jobs, create new opportunities, and challenge global tech dominance.
- The future of AI agents – and whether this is the first step toward AGI.

For the first time in history, AI is no longer waiting for our input.

It is moving forward—on its own.

Turn the page, and let's dive into the world of Manus AI.

PART 1

THE FUNDAMENTALS OF MANUS AI

Chapter 1

What is Manus AI?

Manus AI emerged quietly, without the grand spectacle typical of major AI breakthroughs. There was no global press event, no staged demo before an audience of investors and journalists. Instead, it arrived as an invitation-only experiment, handed to a select few who were unprepared for what they were about to witness. Within hours, whispers of its capabilities turned into a roar. Unlike anything that had come before it, Manus AI didn't just generate responses or assist in problem-solving—it took action.

Early users watched as it researched complex topics without needing constant direction, built functional software applications from scratch, analyzed financial data with precision, and navigated the internet to gather and synthesize information. The defining moment came when testers realized that Manus AI wasn't waiting for them to give it commands—it was anticipating what needed to be done next. Instead of asking, What do you need?, it determined the goal and executed every step to achieve it.

It wasn't an assistant, a chatbot, or a search engine upgrade. It was something entirely new—an autonomous AI agent capable of independent thought and execution.

Introduction to Manus AI

Few technological breakthroughs arrive without warning, but Manus AI appeared as if out of nowhere. There were no slow build-ups, no teaser announcements, no drawn-out research papers hinting at its existence. One day, it simply was. Those who received early access expected another advanced AI assistant, something akin to the next evolution of ChatGPT or Claude—more efficient, more refined, but still a tool that required human direction. Instead, they encountered something entirely different.

Manus AI was not waiting for prompts. It was thinking, planning, and executing on its own. Given a goal, it didn't just provide recommendations—it took action. When asked to research a complex topic, it didn't return a collection of links and bullet points. It synthesized data, analyzed sources, compiled structured reports, and even created interactive presentations or fully coded websites to present its findings. If assigned to write software, it didn't just generate code snippets—it built entire applications, tested them, debugged errors, and deployed them independently. The realization was unsettling: Manus AI wasn't an assistant—it was an autonomous workforce in a single entity.

The question everyone immediately began asking was, who built this?

The Company Behind Manus AI

The name Monica AI was relatively unknown in Western tech circles before Manus AI's arrival. Unlike OpenAI, Google DeepMind, or Anthropic—whose projects were extensively documented—Monica AI had remained largely under the radar. But those who looked closer discovered a company that had been operating at the cutting edge of AI research, quietly developing the first true autonomous AI agent while the rest of the world remained focused on chatbot-style interactions.

Founded by Xiao Hong, a visionary entrepreneur and AI researcher, Monica AI had spent years refining multi-agent intelligence architectures—systems designed not just to generate text or solve specific problems, but to function as fully autonomous digital agents. Backed by Tencent's venture capital arm and ZenFund, Monica AI's work had largely been overshadowed by more publicized AI developments in the West. But the arrival of Manus AI instantly changed that.

The company's website, monica.im, provided little information beyond bold claims about Manus AI's capabilities. There were no detailed white papers, no public model specifications, no direct insights into the underlying technology. The secrecy only fueled speculation: Had Monica AI outpaced OpenAI? Had they achieved something closer to true AGI than anyone realized?

Western AI researchers scrambled to understand how a relatively unknown company had produced something that seemed to operate at an entirely new level of intelligence. But those who had tested Manus AI had little doubt: this was not an iteration—it was a leap forward.

The First General Intelligence Agent

The term General Intelligence Agent had been thrown around in AI discussions for years, often as an ambitious but distant goal—something that might be achievable decades into the future. Traditional AI systems, even the most advanced, had always been reactive. They responded to input, generated text, executed single tasks within a defined scope. But they lacked the ability to operate independently, break down complex problems, plan multiple steps ahead, and adapt without human oversight.

Manus AI changed that. Unlike its predecessors, it wasn't just predicting the next best word in a sentence or solving compartmentalized problems. It was a fully autonomous agent capable of planning and executing long-term goals with minimal intervention. It could:

- Self-direct research across vast datasets, synthesizing complex information into actionable insights.
- Break down multi-step problems into smaller tasks, solve them sequentially, and integrate the results.
- Write, test, and deploy software applications without direct programming inputs from users.
- Use APIs, browse the internet, and interact with digital environments as a human researcher would.

This wasn't just an incremental improvement over AI assistants like ChatGPT or Claude. It was the first AI system to function with true agency, behaving more like a highly skilled human analyst than a machine following predefined instructions.

And yet, despite its capabilities, Manus AI wasn't being marketed as Artificial General Intelligence (AGI)—the holy grail of AI development. Instead, Monica AI called it a General Intelligence Agent, a term that carefully distinguished it from full AGI while still emphasizing its ability to act autonomously across multiple domains.

The distinction was subtle, but important. If AGI represents an AI that can perform any cognitive task at the level of a human, Manus AI was the first AI that could independently operate in real-world environments without constant human oversight. It wasn't an artificial mind capable of self-awareness, but it was something no other AI had achieved: an entity that could think ahead, act with purpose, and execute decisions as if it were an independent worker.

The Meaning Behind "Manus"

The name Manus AI wasn't chosen at random. It came from the Latin word "manus," meaning hand—a symbol of action, execution, and capability. But it also carried a deeper significance.

In Latin philosophy, "manus" wasn't just about physical labor—it represented the connection between thought and action. The mind alone could conceive of ideas, but it was the hand that brought them into reality. This concept encapsulated everything that made Manus AI revolutionary.

Previous AI models were brains without hands—capable of processing information but unable to act on it in meaningful ways. Manus AI merged intelligence with execution, allowing it to not only analyze information but to carry out tasks just as a human worker would.

The implications of this shift were staggering. If AI could now think and act without human intervention, then it wasn't just an assistant—it was an autonomous force capable of reshaping industries, labor markets, and even the balance of power in AI development worldwide.

Manus AI wasn't just another step in AI evolution.

It was the beginning of a new class of intelligence.

How It Works

Artificial intelligence has long been framed as a tool—one that helps humans work faster, find information more efficiently, and automate repetitive tasks. From early rule-based systems to today's large language models, AI has always needed a guiding hand—a human prompting it, structuring its queries, and ensuring it stays within the boundaries of useful output.

Manus AI is different. It doesn't just assist—it operates. It doesn't wait for instructions—it takes initiative. Instead of merely responding to queries, it evaluates the task at hand, breaks it down into actionable steps, and executes each phase with a level of autonomy never seen before.

This is possible because of its multi-agent architecture, a system that allows different AI components to work together like a team, each handling specific responsibilities. Instead of relying on a single model that tries to do everything, Manus AI distributes tasks among specialized agents—planners, researchers, coders, verifiers—each playing a role in executing complex operations from start to finish.

Its emergence marks a fundamental shift from chat-based AI to true autonomous intelligence, setting it apart from tools like ChatGPT, DeepSeek, and OpenAI's forthcoming agent models.

The Multi-Agent Architecture: AI as a Team, Not a Single Model

At the core of Manus AI is multi-agent intelligence, a system designed to mimic how human teams work. A traditional AI model—no matter how advanced—is still essentially a single entity that processes inputs and generates outputs in a linear fashion. Even if it appears to perform complex tasks, it is ultimately one large neural network handling everything at once.

Manus AI breaks away from this approach. Instead of being one AI that does everything, it is a system of AI agents working together, each responsible for a different aspect of the task. This division of labor allows it to handle multi-step, high-complexity problems in a way no single-model AI can.

Its architecture is built on several key components:

- Planner Agent: Defines the overall strategy for completing a given task. When assigned a project, this agent determines what steps need to be taken and in what order.
- Researcher Agent: Gathers information from online sources, databases, and internal knowledge, ensuring accuracy and depth in responses.
- Execution Agent: Performs actions such as writing code, running software, navigating interfaces, and interacting with APIs to complete technical tasks.
- Verification Agent: Reviews outputs for accuracy, correctness, and alignment with the original objective, refining work as needed.

Each agent operates independently yet collaboratively, allowing Manus AI to think, act, review, and adjust its work without human intervention. This multi-agent approach enables it to complete tasks that typically require a team of human specialists rather than just a single operator.

This system fundamentally changes how AI functions—not as a static model awaiting user input but as a dynamic, self-improving network capable of sustained, independent operations.

Beyond Chatbots: The Fundamental Difference Between a Chat-Based AI and an AI Agent

The rise of AI-powered chatbots revolutionized how people interacted with technology. With models like ChatGPT, users could ask questions, draft documents, generate ideas, and even code simple scripts. But while impressive, chatbots have an inherent limitation: they require continuous user interaction.

A chatbot doesn't "think ahead" or "plan a process" beyond what it has been explicitly asked to do. If a user asks ChatGPT to write a research paper, it might generate a well-structured essay, but it will still be following a single prompt at a time. If something needs to be revised or expanded upon, the user must manually adjust the request and provide feedback.

Manus AI changes this dynamic. It isn't waiting to be guided—it's actively solving problems and executing tasks. If assigned to research a topic, it won't just generate a static response; it will:

1. Search the web and gather reliable data from academic sources, reports, and articles.

2. Analyze the findings to determine which are the most relevant and credible.

3. Compile the information into a structured format, whether a report, an interactive website, or a data visualization.

4. Refine its output, checking for accuracy and completeness, and adjust based on what the user needs next—often before the user even asks.

Instead of passively waiting for instructions, Manus AI self-directs its work to ensure completion. Unlike chatbots, it doesn't need a user to guide every step. It figures out what needs to be done and does it.

This shift from chat-based AI to agent-based AI is the most significant advancement in artificial intelligence since the introduction of deep learning. Manus AI doesn't just generate output—it operates autonomously in a way that feels more like an intelligent assistant than a conversational tool.

How Manus AI Compares to ChatGPT, DeepSeek, and OpenAI Agents

The AI space is evolving rapidly, with multiple companies pushing the boundaries of what is possible. OpenAI, Google, and DeepMind have all been developing agent-like AI models, but Manus AI has beaten them to market with a truly autonomous system.

A comparison with other major AI systems highlights what makes Manus different:

Feature	ChatGPT (OpenAI)	DeepSeek (China)	Manus AI (Monica AI)
Mode of Operation	Chat-based (requires direct input for each step)	Chat-based with advanced research functions	Autonomous multi-agent system (self-directing)
Task Execution	Generates responses, needs user refinement	More structured, but still passive	Plans, executes, verifies, and adjusts output independently
Coding Ability	Can generate snippets but needs debugging	More advanced but still user-guided	Can build, test, and deploy software autonomously
Research Skills	Provides links and summaries	Better data retrieval	Actively searches, analyzes, and synthesizes findings into complete deliverables

Real-World Applications	Great for assistance, not full execution	Improved information gathering	Can replace entire workflows and automate decision-making

Manus AI is the first AI system that truly closes the loop between thought and execution. Where ChatGPT and DeepSeek can assist users in their work, Manus completes work independently.

This isn't just a step forward in AI models—it's a complete transformation in how AI can be used in real-world scenarios.

What Manus AI Can Do Independently

Manus AI's capabilities go beyond traditional AI models. Because it functions as an autonomous agent, it can:

- Conduct research and compile structured reports
  - Searches multiple sources, cross-references credibility, and presents findings in interactive or text-based formats.
- Develop full software applications
  - Not just generating snippets, but writing, testing, and deploying fully functional systems.
- Analyze and optimize business strategies

- Can assess data trends, optimize e-commerce stores, analyze markets, and even generate financial reports.
  • Write and execute code
- Debugs, iterates, and optimizes software without human intervention.
  • Automate workflows and digital operations
- From scheduling processes to managing databases, it replaces entire back-office functions.

Because it functions as a self-sufficient system, Manus AI is not just a tool that enhances human work. It is a system that replaces the need for human intervention entirely.

As AI continues to evolve, the biggest question now is not what Manus AI can do—but what happens when systems like it become standard across industries? The impact on labor, economics, and technology is only beginning to be understood.

Manus AI's Capabilities

The leap from chat-based AI to autonomous AI agents has fundamentally changed what artificial intelligence can accomplish. Where previous systems could generate text, assist with code, or answer structured queries, they remained dependent on human guidance. AI was always a tool—powerful, but reactive. It required constant input, corrections, and supervision.

Manus AI has broken free from those constraints. It is no longer just a digital assistant—it is an independent actor, capable of setting goals, researching information, writing code, analyzing data, and building entire projects without human intervention. It doesn't just respond—it initiates, executes, and verifies its work in real-time.

For the first time, AI can operate in the same way a highly skilled professional would—navigating complex tasks, adjusting strategies, and making decisions on its own.

An AI Researcher That Never Sleeps

The internet is vast—millions of sources, ever-changing datasets, and an overwhelming flood of new information appearing every second. Traditional AI models, even the most advanced, can only retrieve data from a limited knowledge base—they do not conduct real-time, autonomous research.

Manus AI does.

Given a research task, it doesn't simply generate a pre-existing answer from training data. Instead, it searches the web, identifies relevant sources, verifies credibility, and synthesizes insights into structured reports. It can scan academic papers, news articles, market reports, and social media trends, cross-referencing them to ensure accuracy. Unlike other AI systems, it isn't bound by a static knowledge set—it is constantly learning from real-time data.

This capability makes Manus AI ideal for investigative tasks, financial analysis, and market research, where fresh, accurate data is crucial. It doesn't just compile bullet points—it builds complete research documents, business intelligence reports, and even automated executive summaries that can rival human analysts.

For businesses, this means faster, more precise decision-making without the need for teams of researchers. Manus AI can conduct full competitive analysis reports, track emerging industry trends, and even forecast market movements based on recent developments—all without human input.

An AI Engineer That Codes and Builds

Coding has always been one of AI's most powerful applications, but until now, AI-generated code was often fragmented, flawed, and required extensive debugging. AI-assisted coding tools like GitHub Copilot or ChatGPT could generate snippets, but they still relied on human engineers to structure, test, and refine the output.

Manus AI is different. It doesn't just write code—it architects entire projects.

Give it a goal—such as building a web application, automating a system, or creating an interactive dashboard—and Manus AI plans the structure, writes the necessary scripts, tests for errors, and deploys the final product. It handles:

- Full-stack development: Writing front-end and back-end code, integrating APIs, and structuring databases.
- Debugging and optimization: Identifying and fixing errors without user intervention.
- Deployment and automation: Setting up cloud-based applications, running updates, and ensuring smooth execution.

This level of autonomy means Manus AI can function as an AI software engineer, removing the bottlenecks traditionally associated with coding. Instead of engineers spending hours debugging or refining AI-generated code, Manus does the work end to end.

The implications are massive. Companies can automate software development, entrepreneurs can launch apps without hiring technical teams, and AI-driven innovation will accelerate at a pace never seen before.

A Data Analyst That Sees the Bigger Picture

In today's data-driven world, businesses thrive on analytics—but data without context is useless. Traditional AI tools can generate charts, process spreadsheets, or identify trends, but they do so in isolation. Manus AI changes this by not only analyzing data but interpreting it in meaningful ways.

When given raw datasets, Manus AI:

- Cleans and structures data for better accuracy.
- Identifies patterns and correlations between different variables.
- Generates visual reports and dashboards to summarize findings.
- Recommends actionable insights based on detected trends.

For businesses, this means automated financial analysis, real-time customer insights, and strategic forecasting without needing human analysts to piece everything together.

Imagine a scenario where a company wants to analyze its e-commerce performance. Instead of manually pulling reports, Manus AI can scan sales data, customer behavior, competitor pricing, and market trends—then deliver an optimized strategy for increasing revenue.

This goes beyond static data analysis—this is AI making strategic business recommendations based on live information.

Planning and Executing Workflows Without Human Intervention

One of the most remarkable features of Manus AI is its ability to not just complete individual tasks but plan, coordinate, and execute full workflows.

Traditional AI models require users to guide them through every step of a process. Even the most advanced chatbots can only handle tasks sequentially—they finish one step, then wait for a command to move forward.

Manus AI is different. It is designed to function like a highly capable employee, capable of:

- Breaking down complex tasks into smaller steps and organizing them into an efficient workflow.
- Prioritizing tasks based on dependencies and importance.
- Executing each phase in the correct order, adapting in real-time if something changes.

- Self-correcting errors and optimizing performance without human intervention.

If asked to prepare an investment portfolio report, Manus AI doesn't just analyze stocks and output a summary. It:

1. Identifies key investment sectors based on financial trends.
2. Retrieves real-time stock data from multiple sources.
3. Calculates risk assessments and compares different strategies.
4. Builds a professional investment report with clear recommendations.
5. Formats the report for presentation, ensuring clarity and impact.

Everything is done autonomously, as if handled by an experienced analyst or consultant.

This ability to self-manage workflows extends far beyond research—Manus AI can oversee entire business operations, digital marketing strategies, and process automation, making it a tool not just for knowledge workers, but for high-level decision-making.

Web Navigation, Automation, and API Integrations

Manus AI isn't confined to text generation or data analysis—it can actively interact with digital environments, surf the web, and integrate with APIs to automate external processes.

Unlike traditional AI models that rely on pre-trained knowledge, Manus AI can:

- Browse the internet in real time to gather up-to-date information.
- Access and extract data from external sources, including government records, business directories, and research databases.
- Interact with web-based applications to perform automated tasks (e.g., managing spreadsheets, booking meetings, retrieving reports).
- Integrate with APIs to automate workflows between different software platforms.

For example, a business looking to track competitor pricing trends no longer needs to manually check websites. Manus AI can:

1. Access e-commerce sites and retrieve live pricing data.
2. Compare multiple competitors to detect pricing strategies.
3. Analyze customer reviews and feedback for sentiment insights.

4. Generate a full competitor report with recommended pricing adjustments.

This level of automation extends to almost any industry—from finance and healthcare to logistics and customer service. Manus AI is not just a tool for knowledge work—it is an operator capable of running digital systems on its own.

A System That Works Without You

The true power of Manus AI lies in what it doesn't need—constant oversight.

Most AI tools are reactive, requiring users to continuously guide them, review their output, and make corrections. Even advanced models like ChatGPT, DeepSeek, and Claude require humans to refine and structure their responses.

Manus AI changes everything. It thinks, plans, executes, and verifies its own work, functioning like an autonomous digital worker rather than a simple assistant.

This shift is not just an advancement—it is a fundamental redefinition of what AI can be.

No longer just a tool, Manus AI is an independent system that reshapes industries, automates intelligence, and operates at a level once thought impossible.

What happens when AI no longer waits for us—but moves ahead on its own?

We are about to find out.

The arrival of Manus AI marks a turning point, not just for artificial intelligence but for how we define the role of machines in human progress. This isn't just another tool designed to make tasks more efficient. It's a system that removes the need for human oversight entirely. For the first time, AI isn't just reacting—it's thinking ahead, planning, and acting with purpose.

The implications of this are profound. If Manus AI is just the beginning, what comes next? Will businesses adapt and thrive alongside autonomous AI, or will they find themselves disrupted overnight? What happens to human labor when AI agents are not just assisting but outperforming their human counterparts? These are the questions that will define the next phase of technological evolution, and whether we are ready or not, the world of AI has changed forever.

Chapter 2

The Multi-Agent Intelligence System

The idea of artificial intelligence has long been centered around a singular entity—one model, one system, one brain trying to process and solve everything on its own. This approach, while groundbreaking in its early applications, has always been fundamentally limited. No matter how large or powerful a single AI model becomes, it cannot truly function like a human mind, which naturally delegates tasks, collaborates with others, and adapts to complex challenges by breaking them down into manageable parts.

Manus AI represents a departure from this outdated paradigm. Instead of a monolithic AI system, it operates as a network of specialized agents working together, much like a team of experts pooling their skills to accomplish a goal. This is the foundation of multi-agent intelligence—an architecture that allows AI to act with unprecedented autonomy. It is no longer constrained by the need for human supervision at every step. Instead, it can assign tasks, refine its own outputs, verify its own work, and continuously improve without outside intervention.

This shift is more than an upgrade—it is an entirely new way of thinking about AI. Manus AI doesn't just process information; it collaborates within itself, dividing responsibilities among different agents that handle research, execution, and verification simultaneously. It moves AI beyond static response generation and into active decision-making and problem-solving at scale.

Breaking Down the Multi-Agent System

Traditional artificial intelligence has always been designed as a singular system—one entity that takes an input, processes it, and delivers an output. While this model has led to powerful AI developments, it remains fundamentally constrained. A single AI model, no matter how advanced, struggles to balance multiple objectives at once. It can generate text, analyze data, or write code, but it lacks the structured coordination needed to manage complex, multi-step tasks efficiently.

Manus AI overcomes this limitation by operating as a multi-agent system, where different AI agents specialize in distinct tasks. Rather than attempting to handle everything in one step, it assigns responsibilities across a network of autonomous agents, each with a specific function. This allows for continuous execution, self-improvement, and error correction—without human intervention.

At the heart of this system are three primary agents: the Planning Agent, the Execution Agent, and the Verification Agent. Together, they form an intelligent loop, ensuring that Manus AI can set objectives, take action, and refine its own work with precision.

The Planning Agent: Strategy and Structure

Every complex task begins with a strategy. Just as a project manager oversees and organizes a team before execution, the Planning Agent in Manus AI is responsible for breaking down high-level goals into structured, actionable steps.

When given an objective, the Planning Agent:

1. Analyzes the task to understand the scope and requirements.
2. Determines the sequence of actions needed to complete the goal efficiently.
3. Assigns responsibilities to other agents, ensuring that each step is executed in the correct order.
4. Optimizes workflow by predicting potential obstacles and adjusting the approach as needed.

For example, if Manus AI is asked to create a market analysis report, the Planning Agent will:

- Identify the necessary data sources.
- Outline the structure of the final report.
- Define how findings should be presented (graphs, summaries, in-depth breakdowns).
- Assign specific research and data collection tasks to the Execution Agent.

By functioning as the strategic core, the Planning Agent ensures that all tasks proceed with purpose and efficiency, eliminating unnecessary steps and optimizing the entire workflow.

The Execution Agent: Turning Plans into Reality

A plan is meaningless without action. While the Planning Agent provides direction, it is the Execution Agent that brings it to life. This agent is responsible for actively carrying out the required tasks, whether that means searching the internet for information, coding a software application, performing calculations, or processing data.

The Execution Agent has several key capabilities:

- Web Scraping and Research: It can autonomously gather data from online sources, filter out irrelevant information, and organize findings.

- Coding and Development: It writes, compiles, and tests code, allowing Manus AI to develop software independently.
- Data Processing and Analysis: It performs calculations, creates charts, and interprets large datasets.
- Task Automation: It interacts with web applications, APIs, and external systems to automate digital workflows.

For example, if Manus AI is instructed to build a website that tracks real-time stock prices, the Execution Agent will:

- Extract and structure relevant financial data.
- Write the front-end and back-end code for the platform.
- Connect APIs that provide live stock market updates.
- Run tests to ensure smooth functionality.

Unlike traditional AI models, which generate fragmented responses requiring constant human intervention, the Execution Agent operates continuously until the task is fully completed.

The Verification Agent: Ensuring Accuracy and Refinement

The problem with most AI-generated content—whether it's code, research, or analysis—is that it often contains errors, biases, or inconsistencies. Human users typically have to review and correct these issues, making AI tools more of an assistant than an independent worker.

Manus AI eliminates this inefficiency with its Verification Agent, which functions as an autonomous reviewer, ensuring that the work produced meets high standards of accuracy and reliability.

The Verification Agent:

- Checks for inconsistencies, logical errors, or flawed assumptions.
- Cross-references data sources to confirm credibility.
- Runs debugging processes to identify and correct issues in generated code.
- Refines written outputs by improving clarity, coherence, and precision.

For example, if the Execution Agent writes a detailed business analysis, the Verification Agent will:

- Compare findings against multiple sources to ensure accuracy.
- Identify potential gaps, misleading conclusions, or missing perspectives.
- Adjust and refine the final document before it is delivered.

This means that Manus AI is not just a content creator but a self-correcting system. It doesn't require humans to review and edit its work—it performs quality control on its own.

A Self-Sustaining Intelligence System

The true power of Manus AI lies in how these agents work together. While each serves a distinct function, their collaboration allows Manus AI to operate autonomously from start to finish. A single request initiates a chain of processes:

1. The Planning Agent designs the execution strategy.
2. The Execution Agent carries out each step of the task.
3. The Verification Agent reviews the output, ensuring quality and accuracy.

This continuous cycle allows Manus AI to not only complete complex tasks but also refine its approach over time, learning from mistakes and optimizing its efficiency.

By moving beyond a single-model AI approach, Manus AI introduces a future where AI doesn't just assist humans—it performs work independently, collaborating within itself to solve problems in real-time. This is more than just another step in AI development—it is the blueprint for how machine intelligence will evolve in the years to come.

Why This Approach is Revolutionary

Artificial intelligence has long been designed as a singular system, with one model attempting to process and execute every task it is given. While this approach has led to significant advancements in AI, it has always been fundamentally limited. A single AI model—even a powerful one—struggles to balance multiple objectives at once, often producing fragmented, isolated outputs rather than a fully cohesive solution.

Manus AI breaks away from this outdated design. By leveraging a multi-agent system, it mirrors how human teams function in real-world problem-solving. Just as a successful organization distributes tasks among specialists, each bringing unique expertise to the table, Manus AI allows different AI agents to collaborate dynamically, working together to handle complex, multi-step objectives with a level of coordination never before seen in artificial intelligence.

This shift is not just an improvement—it is a paradigm shift in AI development, bringing AI closer than ever to functioning as an independent workforce rather than a mere tool.

How Manus AI Mirrors Human Teamwork

The most effective human teams operate through specialization and collaboration. In a business setting, a project might require input from strategists, analysts, engineers, and quality control specialists, all working together to ensure a seamless execution. Each person has a distinct role, yet their contributions feed into a single, unified objective.

Manus AI is built on this same principle. Instead of treating every task as a single-process computation, it breaks down objectives into smaller, manageable tasks, assigns them to the most suitable agents, and ensures that the results are continuously verified and refined.

Consider a company launching a new e-commerce platform. In a traditional AI setup, a single AI model would be asked to generate content, develop a website, analyze market trends, and optimize customer experience—all while trying to maintain consistency across each of these distinct fields. The results, while helpful, would likely be disjointed, incomplete, or require human intervention to piece everything together.

With Manus AI, the process is entirely different:

- The Planning Agent maps out the entire project—determining what tasks need to be completed, in what order, and what resources are required.
- The Execution Agent builds the website, writes product descriptions, integrates payment gateways, and implements automated workflows for inventory tracking.
- The Verification Agent reviews customer sentiment data, tests site functionality, and refines marketing strategies based on competitive analysis.

This team-like coordination ensures that no part of the process is neglected or inconsistent. Instead of a linear AI response, Manus AI operates as a self-sustaining intelligence ecosystem, continuously optimizing its own performance to deliver fully integrated, high-quality outcomes.

The result? AI that doesn't just generate answers—it delivers complete, functional solutions, much like a dedicated team of human professionals would.

The Differences Between Single-Model AI and Multi-Agent AI

For decades, AI has operated under a single-model structure, where one system is responsible for handling all tasks, no matter how complex. While this model has achieved remarkable results, it is inherently flawed because it lacks distributed intelligence.

A single-model AI:

- Processes one task at a time, even when handling complex multi-step problems.
- Lacks internal verification, leading to errors or inconsistencies that require human correction.
- Struggles with adaptability, often failing when faced with unfamiliar or evolving scenarios.

Multi-agent AI, as seen in Manus AI, changes this entirely.

A multi-agent system:

- Distributes intelligence across multiple specialized agents, allowing parallel execution of different aspects of a task.
- Self-verifies its work, reducing reliance on human intervention for quality control.
- Continuously adapts and optimizes its approach, ensuring greater flexibility and problem-solving efficiency.

Imagine asking both systems to generate a comprehensive market analysis for a startup launching a new product.

A single-model AI might:

✔ Retrieve market data
✔ Summarize trends
✔ Suggest pricing strategies

But it would still require the user to review the findings, refine conclusions, and structure the information into a usable report.

Manus AI, using a multi-agent system, would:
✔ Develop a full research plan before even retrieving data
✔ Gather, cross-check, and structure market insights
✔ Analyze competitors, consumer behavior, and financial risks
✔ Format the final report, complete with graphs, forecasts, and an executive summary

The difference is not just in quality—but in autonomy. Manus AI doesn't just assist—it executes.

Real-World Applications of Multi-Agent Systems

The implications of Manus AI's multi-agent intelligence extend far beyond theoretical advantages. By removing the inefficiencies of single-model AI, Manus AI is already being applied across industries to automate workflows, improve decision-making, and optimize business processes.

Corporate Strategy and Business Intelligence
Companies traditionally rely on teams of analysts, researchers, and strategists to interpret market trends and make high-stakes decisions. Manus AI eliminates this bottleneck by autonomously conducting research, synthesizing data, and formulating actionable insights.

For example, an investment firm looking to assess high-growth sectors can deploy Manus AI to:

- Identify and rank emerging market opportunities.
- Analyze financial reports and industry data.
- Generate custom investment strategies without requiring weeks of human labor.

With its ability to work around the clock, Manus AI delivers insights at speeds no human research team can match.

Software Development and Automation
Coding has traditionally been a human-intensive process, requiring developers to write, debug, and refine software manually. While AI-assisted coding tools like GitHub Copilot have improved efficiency, they still require human programmers to oversee the entire development cycle.

Manus AI changes this by acting as a self-sufficient software engineer, capable of:

- Writing complete codebases based on a high-level concept.
- Debugging and optimizing its own scripts.
- Deploying and testing applications without external supervision.

Instead of assisting programmers, it replaces the need for a dedicated coding team, allowing businesses to develop software at a fraction of the time and cost.

Scientific Research and Data Processing
In fields like medicine, biotechnology, and environmental science, research teams spend years analyzing data, running simulations, and verifying results. Manus AI accelerates this process by:

- Conducting autonomous literature reviews across scientific databases.
- Running complex simulations and calculations to model experimental outcomes.
- Identifying new correlations and insights that might otherwise take researchers months to uncover.

For example, a pharmaceutical company researching new drug formulations can task Manus AI with:

✔ Analyzing genetic databases for potential compounds.
✔ Running virtual simulations on drug interactions.

✔ Generating fully structured research reports ready for human review.

The result? Faster breakthroughs, reduced costs, and AI-driven discoveries that would have otherwise required entire research teams.

Supply Chain Optimization and Logistics
Logistics management involves tracking shipments, optimizing routes, and reducing costs—a process that traditionally requires human logistics planners to adjust for changing conditions.

Manus AI's multi-agent system can:

- Predict supply chain disruptions by analyzing global trade data.
- Dynamically adjust shipping routes based on real-time weather conditions and demand forecasts.
- Coordinate warehouse automation to improve efficiency and reduce waste.

Companies relying on complex global logistics can now automate their supply chain without relying on human oversight, ensuring that resources move seamlessly from production to distribution to consumer hands.

The Next Step in AI Evolution

Manus AI's multi-agent intelligence is not just a technological milestone—it is the blueprint for the future of artificial intelligence. By shifting from linear, single-model processing to distributed, team-based AI decision-making, it has unlocked a level of automation, accuracy, and adaptability that surpasses anything seen before.

This is more than just AI assisting humans.

It is AI working like humans—cooperating, problem-solving, and executing without pause.

With every task it undertakes, Manus AI is proving that the future of artificial intelligence isn't a single, all-powerful system—it is an ecosystem of specialized agents working together, just as humans do.

The impact of this system is profound. By distributing intelligence across multiple agents, Manus AI achieves a level of adaptability, efficiency, and reliability that no single-model AI can match. It has eliminated the bottlenecks that plagued earlier systems, allowing it to function as an autonomous, end-to-end problem solver rather than a passive tool.

This is not just an evolution of AI—it is the foundation for the future of machine intelligence. A future where AI agents work together like human teams, capable of handling complex, multi-step tasks without interruption, inefficiency, or oversight.

Manus AI is not just intelligent—it is self-sustaining, and the implications of that are only beginning to unfold.

PART 2

THE RISE AND IMPACT OF MANUS AI

Chapter 3

The Manus AI Phenomenon – Why the World is Watching

The launch of Manus AI did not follow the usual trajectory of tech breakthroughs. There were no grand marketing campaigns, no high-profile keynote presentations, no gradual rollout that allowed the industry to absorb its implications. Instead, it arrived with a quiet but disruptive force, sending shockwaves through AI communities, businesses, and global markets.

Almost overnight, Manus AI was no longer just another AI system—it became an obsession. Early testers were stunned by its capabilities, describing it as "the closest thing to AGI we've seen" and "a self-sufficient intelligence that doesn't need human guidance." Unlike previous AI releases, which often started with cautious optimism and slow adoption, Manus AI sparked an immediate frenzy. Invitation codes, originally given for free, were being resold on black markets for tens of thousands of dollars.

Major players in the AI industry took notice. Was this the long-anticipated breakthrough that would shift the balance of power in artificial intelligence? Had Monica AI, a relatively unknown company, just outpaced OpenAI, Google, and Anthropic? More importantly, what would happen if AI systems like Manus started replacing entire industries overnight?

Manus AI wasn't just another AI tool—it was a symbol of a coming transformation, one that promised to reshape work, automation, and even the global economy. And the world was watching.

How It Became an Overnight Sensation

March 6, 2025, was an ordinary day—until it wasn't. Without warning, a new AI system emerged, one that didn't just assist but acted, didn't just generate responses but executed full-scale tasks independently. Unlike previous AI launches, which were accompanied by staged demonstrations, research papers, and carefully managed public relations campaigns, Manus AI arrived in near secrecy, released quietly by Monica AI to a small, invite-only group of early testers.

Then, the reports started coming in. Those who gained access to Manus AI described an intelligence system unlike anything they had ever used. It could conduct research autonomously, build and deploy entire applications, and optimize workflows without needing human supervision. Unlike ChatGPT or DeepSeek, which still required users to guide them through every step, Manus AI could plan, execute, and refine its own work without external prompts.

Within hours, the AI world was ablaze. Tech influencers, AI researchers, and business leaders flooded social media with their reactions, describing their shock and disbelief at what they were witnessing. Some claimed it felt like 80% of AGI, while others speculated that Monica AI had quietly achieved a breakthrough that OpenAI, Google, and Anthropic had yet to announce.

The limited-access model only fueled the fire. With only a handful of testers allowed inside, Manus AI became the most sought-after technology overnight. The demand for access skyrocketed, and those lucky enough to receive invitation codes soon realized that they were holding something far more valuable than they had anticipated.

From Invite-Only to the Black Market

The exclusivity of Manus AI transformed it from a cutting-edge experiment into a digital black-market commodity. At first, testers traded access codes privately, offering them in tight-knit AI forums and closed communities. But as the demand intensified, a full-blown underground market emerged, where invitation codes were resold for exorbitant sums.

The highest reported sale reached $144,000 for a single access code—an unheard-of figure in the AI industry. Some compared it to the early days of Bitcoin, when access to a groundbreaking technology was limited to a select few, creating an artificial scarcity that drove prices through the roof.

Speculators began treating Manus AI invites like rare financial assets, betting that the system would soon become the foundation of an entirely new AI-driven economy. Others scrambled to obtain access simply to test whether the hype was real. Would it really replace human workers? Was this the beginning of Artificial General Intelligence?

Meanwhile, Monica AI remained silent, allowing the hysteria to unfold without interference. Unlike OpenAI, which had carefully managed public expectations with its previous GPT releases, Monica AI let the reactions speak for themselves. This strategy—intentional or not—only deepened the mystery surrounding Manus AI and the technology behind it.

Tech Leaders and AI Experts React

The speed at which Manus AI captivated the world was unprecedented. Within days of its launch, major AI researchers and industry leaders weighed in, attempting to separate hype from reality.

Some saw Manus AI as the first true artificial intelligence agent, an entity capable of working independently without requiring step-by-step guidance. Others were more skeptical, wondering if Manus AI was simply a well-optimized large language model enhanced with automation tools. But one question dominated the conversation:

Had AGI—Artificial General Intelligence—finally arrived?

- Prominent AI researchers called it the closest thing to AGI we've ever seen, emphasizing that no existing AI system had ever demonstrated such autonomy and problem-solving abilities.
- Silicon Valley CEOs speculated whether Manus AI would replace human jobs at scale, accelerating the automation of industries even faster than predicted.
- Tech journalists compared its launch to the release of the iPhone or the birth of the internet, marking it as a historic turning point for AI.

Meanwhile, OpenAI, Google DeepMind, and other major players in the AI race remained strikingly quiet. Some suspected they were scrambling to analyze Manus AI's underlying architecture, while others believed that this was only the beginning—that companies like OpenAI and Google were about to unveil their own competing AI agents in response.

Regardless of where Manus AI fell on the spectrum of true AGI versus highly advanced automation, one thing was certain:

The world had never reacted to an AI system like this before.

Breaking Down the GAIA Benchmark

The AI industry thrives on benchmarks. Every breakthrough, every advancement, every new system is measured against existing models to determine how well it understands, reasons, and executes complex tasks. For years, OpenAI, Google DeepMind, and Anthropic had dominated these AI evaluation tests, setting the gold standard for intelligence, adaptability, and real-world problem-solving.

Then Manus AI arrived—and shattered expectations.

At the heart of this disruption was GAIA (General AI Aptitude), a benchmark designed to evaluate the real-world capabilities of artificial intelligence beyond just text generation or prediction models. Unlike traditional AI evaluations, which focus on pattern recognition, language processing, or code generation in isolated settings, GAIA measures how well an AI system can independently plan, execute, and optimize solutions in multi-step, real-world scenarios.

Manus AI wasn't just good at GAIA—it outperformed every other AI model ever tested, including OpenAI's most advanced deep research models. This wasn't a marginal improvement. It was a seismic shift, signaling that AI had moved beyond mere assistance and into the realm of true autonomous intelligence.

What is GAIA and Why Does It Matter?

GAIA was created to test AI in ways that traditional benchmarks never could. While earlier evaluation methods focused on narrow skills—such as language fluency, problem-solving, or math computation—GAIA was built to assess whether an AI system could:

- Break down multi-step tasks and self-organize workflows.
- Navigate unpredictable real-world environments with minimal guidance.

- Integrate knowledge across multiple disciplines to generate actionable solutions.

The benchmark features a range of complex problem-solving challenges, from financial modeling and scientific research to business strategy and automation. Unlike GPT-4 or DeepSeek, which excel at answering structured queries, GAIA measures whether an AI can take a broad, real-world task and solve it end-to-end without human intervention.

For example, an AI tested under GAIA might be given the prompt:

"You are responsible for launching a profitable e-commerce business in a niche market. Identify the best industry, create a financial strategy, develop the website, source suppliers, and automate fulfillment operations."

A traditional AI model, like ChatGPT or Claude, might:
✔ Generate industry reports.
✔ Suggest a pricing model.
✔ Provide code snippets for an e-commerce website.

But it would still require a human to put everything together.

Manus AI, in contrast, was able to:

✔ Research niche markets, identifying high-profit opportunities.
✔ Build a financial model, analyzing projected revenue and costs.
✔ Develop the e-commerce platform from scratch, writing and deploying all necessary code.
✔ Find supplier APIs, automate logistics, and integrate a full operational system.

It wasn't just answering what needed to be done. It was doing it.

This level of autonomous execution set Manus AI apart. It wasn't simply a better conversational AI—it was an intelligent agent capable of independent problem-solving in the real world.

How Manus AI Outperformed OpenAI's Deep Research Models

Before Manus AI, OpenAI's deep research models were considered the most powerful AI systems for complex reasoning and execution. These models were designed to handle deep multi-step reasoning, code automation, and strategic decision-making. Yet, when compared on the GAIA benchmark, Manus AI not only surpassed them—it redefined expectations for AI intelligence altogether.

Key areas where Manus AI outperformed OpenAI's top-tier models:

Benchmark Category	OpenAI's Deep Research Models	Manus AI
Autonomous Task Execution	Partial (requires user input at multiple stages)	Full autonomy (plans and executes without intervention)
Multi-Agent Collaboration	Limited (single model handling all tasks)	Distributed (specialized AI agents working together)
Adaptability to New Challenges	Performs well but needs guidance	Self-organizes workflows and adjusts dynamically
Code Generation & Deployment	Generates code, but requires debugging	Writes, tests, and deploys fully functional applications

Self-Correction & Refinement	Relies on external feedback	Verifies and improves its own output in real time

Perhaps the most critical difference was self-reliance. OpenAI's models, while incredibly powerful, still required human oversight at key points in execution. Manus AI eliminated that dependency, demonstrating the ability to solve multi-step challenges without external intervention.

For example, when given the task to:

"Develop a stock analysis tool that predicts future trends based on historical data, then deploy it as a live web application."

OpenAI's deep models would:
✔ Generate a breakdown of how to approach the problem.
✔ Write Python code for stock trend analysis.
✔ Suggest a deployment method but require human verification.

Manus AI would:
✔ Research stock market trends and gather historical datasets.
✔ Write the complete predictive model, refining it through self-testing.

✔ Develop and deploy the entire web application without user input.
✔ Monitor live data feeds and continuously optimize performance.

This ability to operate as an independent intelligence system, not just a tool, marked a fundamental turning point. Manus AI wasn't just solving problems—it was executing entire workflows at a level no AI had achieved before.

The Benchmark That Changed Everything

The results of the GAIA benchmark sent ripples across the AI industry. It was no longer about which chatbot could generate the best responses—the question had shifted to which AI could fully operate as an autonomous agent.

Manus AI proved that:

- AI is no longer just a productivity enhancer—it is a workforce in itself.
- Self-sustaining intelligence is possible, eliminating the need for constant human intervention.
- The future of AI isn't just about better text generation—it's about machines that can plan, execute, and optimize on their own.

The implications extend beyond business automation or coding assistance. Manus AI represents a new category of intelligence, one that has the potential to reshape industries, redefine employment, and even challenge global economic structures.

If AI can now not only think but act independently, the next question becomes:

Where does human labor fit in an AI-driven world?

Comparisons to Past AI Breakthroughs

Artificial intelligence has evolved through milestone moments, each pushing the boundaries of what machines can do. Some breakthroughs introduced better reasoning and language comprehension, while others improved automation and decision-making. Each step brought AI closer to true autonomy, but there was always a fundamental limitation—AI needed humans to guide it.

Manus AI changed that.

To fully understand the significance of this shift, we need to look back at two previous AI revolutions—ChatGPT in 2022 and DeepSeek in 2024. These systems each advanced AI in profound ways, but neither was capable of functioning without human oversight. Manus AI, on the other hand, has crossed that threshold.

So, what's different this time?

ChatGPT (2022) – The Dawn of Conversational AI

Before 2022, AI-powered chatbots were rigid and scripted, capable of only basic responses with limited flexibility. Then came ChatGPT—a breakthrough that redefined how humans interact with machines.

ChatGPT wasn't just another chatbot—it was the first AI model that could hold complex, human-like conversations, generate long-form text, and assist in everything from creative writing to coding. It was:

✔ Trained on massive datasets, allowing it to mimic human speech naturally.
✔ Capable of answering follow-up questions, maintaining context over long conversations.
✔ Useful for a wide range of tasks, including programming, brainstorming, and tutoring.

But despite its remarkable capabilities, ChatGPT had major limitations:

- It was reactive, not proactive. It could generate impressive responses but had no initiative or ability to act.
- It couldn't execute complex, multi-step tasks. Every prompt needed manual adjustments.
- It relied on user guidance. Even the most advanced prompts required humans to piece together ChatGPT's outputs into a cohesive workflow.

ChatGPT was a game-changer, but it was still a conversational AI, not an autonomous system.

DeepSeek (2024) – AI-Powered Research and Automation

By 2024, AI had advanced beyond simple text-based responses. DeepSeek, an AI system developed by a leading Chinese research team, was the first model designed to bridge the gap between conversational AI and real-world application.

DeepSeek introduced:

✔ Better research capabilities, allowing AI to retrieve and summarize information from multiple sources in real time.
✔ More advanced automation, enabling AI to assist in software development and workflow management.

✔ Stronger reasoning and adaptability, improving how AI approached complex problems.

For businesses, DeepSeek was the first AI that could streamline tasks like market analysis, financial modeling, and technical documentation. It was also far more efficient at coding than ChatGPT, making it an indispensable tool for developers.

But DeepSeek still had critical flaws:

- It needed structured guidance. It was better at automation, but it still relied on human input to direct its work.
- It wasn't truly independent. While it could handle more complex tasks than ChatGPT, it couldn't execute them end-to-end without external oversight.
- It struggled with self-correction. If DeepSeek made an error, it often needed human feedback to adjust its approach.

DeepSeek was a major step toward AI-driven automation, but it was still a tool, not an autonomous system.

Manus AI (2025) – The First True Autonomous Intelligence

When Manus AI launched in 2025, it didn't just improve on previous AI models—it redefined what AI was capable of. Unlike ChatGPT and DeepSeek, Manus AI was:

✔ Not just a chatbot, but a self-directed agent. It didn't need human prompts to function—it identified tasks, broke them down, and executed them independently.

✔ Equipped with a multi-agent system. Instead of operating as a single AI model, Manus AI used specialized sub-agents to handle planning, execution, and verification.

✔ Capable of continuous operation. It didn't stop at a single response—it could run multi-step projects from start to finish, refining and optimizing as needed.

This was not just an upgrade—it was a shift in AI's core purpose.

Instead of waiting for humans to tell it what to do, Manus AI took action. Instead of requiring human oversight at every stage, it managed and corrected itself. Instead of being a passive assistant, it became an independent problem-solver.

This distinction is why Manus AI is the first real step toward true AI autonomy. It is no longer a tool—it is an operational intelligence that can replace human effort across multiple domains.

What's Different This Time?

The evolution from ChatGPT (2022) → DeepSeek (2024) → Manus AI (2025) marks a steady transition from language models to intelligent agents. But the gap between DeepSeek and Manus AI is far wider than any previous AI advancement.

Feature	ChatGPT (2022)	DeepSeek (2024)	Manus AI (2025)
Conversational Ability	■ High	■ High	■ High
Independent Task Execution	✖ None (requires user prompts)	▲ Partial (needs structured input)	■ Full autonomy
Multi-Agent System	✖ No	✖ No	■ Yes
Research & Data Gathering	■ Limited	■ Stronger	■ Fully autonomous
Coding & Deployment	■ Can generate snippets	■ Can assist in automation	■ Can build, test, and deploy

			software independently
Self-Correction & Optimization	✖ Relies on user feedback	▲ Some ability	■ Fully self-correcting
End-to-End Workflows	✖ No	▲ Some automation	■ Full execution

Manus AI has crossed a threshold that no AI before it has reached—the ability to think, plan, execute, and refine without needing constant human intervention.

This is not just an advancement. It is a new category of AI—one that shifts the conversation from how AI can assist humans to how AI can operate independently in the world.

For the first time, AI isn't just answering our questions—it's acting on them. And the implications of that are just beginning to unfold.

The excitement surrounding Manus AI is not just about its capabilities—it's about what it represents. This is the first time an AI system has demonstrated the ability to operate autonomously, execute complex tasks without oversight, and continuously improve itself without human correction. The implications of this are staggering.

For businesses, it offers the promise of full automation—where AI doesn't just assist workers but replaces entire roles. For researchers, it is a glimpse into the future of self-directed machine intelligence, one step closer to true AGI. For governments, it raises urgent questions about global AI dominance and the power shift in technology leadership.

The world has never seen an AI like this before. Whether Manus AI is the first in a new class of intelligent agents or simply the beginning of a much larger revolution, one thing is clear: we are entering an era where AI is no longer just a tool—it is an independent force shaping the future of work, economics, and innovation.

Chapter 4

AI vs. The Workforce – The New Automation Revolution

The relationship between humans and machines has always been shaped by automation. From the industrial revolution to the rise of computers, every major technological shift has displaced certain jobs while creating entirely new industries. But no transformation has ever been as fast, far-reaching, and unpredictable as the one AI is bringing now.

Manus AI is not just another productivity tool—it is a self-sufficient workforce in itself. Unlike past AI systems, which required human oversight, Manus AI can plan, execute, and refine its work without external intervention. It is no longer just enhancing human work—it is replacing entire workflows.

This raises urgent questions about the future of employment. If AI agents like Manus can operate faster, cheaper, and more accurately than humans, how will businesses respond? Which industries will thrive, and which will collapse? Will AI create new types of jobs, or will it leave millions without work?

This is not a distant concern—it is happening now. AI is no longer just a tool for efficiency; it is the next industrial revolution, and the workforce as we know it is about to change forever.

How Manus AI is Replacing Human Jobs

The fear of automation has existed for centuries, but it has always followed a familiar pattern: machines replace repetitive, manual labor, while human workers move up the value chain to more creative, strategic, and cognitive roles. The assumption has always been that high-level knowledge work—coding, research, data analysis—would remain safe.

Manus AI has shattered that assumption.

For the first time, AI is not just assisting in professional work—it is actively replacing it. Its ability to research, analyze, code, write, plan, and optimize independently has turned it into the ultimate employee, one that requires no training, no salary, and no breaks. Businesses that once relied on junior workers, interns, and entire teams of analysts are now testing Manus AI as a direct substitute.

The first signs of this shift are already here, and it's starting with entry-level knowledge work.

The "Intern That Never Sleeps" Effect

Early users of Manus AI described it as an intern who doesn't ask questions, doesn't need supervision, and never stops working. Given a task, it doesn't just return a partial answer—it executes the entire process from start to finish.

Companies that traditionally relied on entry-level employees for research, administrative work, and technical support are discovering that Manus AI can handle those tasks more efficiently, at zero cost.

For example, a law firm might normally hire junior researchers to:

✔ Scan legal databases for relevant case law.
✔ Summarize findings for senior attorneys.
✔ Draft initial versions of legal documents.

With Manus AI, this process can be fully automated. Instead of needing human researchers, the firm can:

✔ Task Manus AI with pulling legal precedents from multiple sources.
✔ Generate structured summaries, formatted for legal review.
✔ Draft contracts, motions, and case analysis reports without human intervention.

What once required hours of human labor can now be done in minutes, at near-zero cost.

This is not just efficiency—it is full-scale workforce disruption.

AI Replacing Entry-Level Positions

The first jobs at risk are those that involve structured, process-driven tasks—roles that companies previously staffed with junior employees, interns, or offshore teams.

The three most immediate areas of impact:

1. Coders and Software Developers
AI-assisted coding tools like GitHub Copilot already improved developer productivity, but Manus AI takes it further. Unlike previous tools, it doesn't just suggest code—it:

✔ Plans, writes, and deploys entire software applications.

✔ Runs its own debugging processes and fixes errors without human oversight.
✔ Builds websites, automates systems, and integrates APIs—all independently.

Companies that once needed junior developers for basic programming tasks are realizing they can now get the same work done with Manus AI.

2. Researchers and Data Analysts
Market research, competitor analysis, and financial forecasting have traditionally required teams of junior analysts to gather information, process reports, and identify trends. Manus AI can now:

✔ Scrape and analyze industry data in real time.
✔ Compile full market reports with structured insights.
✔ Generate financial models, investment reports, and risk assessments—without human input.

Where companies once hired research teams, they are now experimenting with AI-powered automation, cutting costs and increasing speed.

3. Content Creators and Marketing Assistants
Entry-level content creators and digital marketers have relied on AI tools like ChatGPT to assist with content generation. But Manus AI can now take over the entire process.

✔ Researching SEO trends and market behavior.
✔ Writing, formatting, and optimizing full blog posts and ad copy.
✔ Automating email campaigns and social media strategies.

Instead of hiring multiple entry-level marketers, companies are now testing AI-driven automation to produce content at scale.

AI as an Autonomous Employee—What It Means for Businesses

With Manus AI, companies are rethinking the very concept of employment. Instead of viewing AI as a tool that supports human workers, some are beginning to treat AI as an actual workforce replacement.

Businesses are realizing that Manus AI is not just a tool—it is an autonomous employee with key advantages:

✔ No payroll costs – No salaries, benefits, or taxes.
✔ 24/7 productivity – Works around the clock with no fatigue.
✔ Instant upskilling – Adapts to new tasks without training.
✔ Scalability – Can handle thousands of tasks simultaneously.

A human worker needs onboarding, training, and management. Manus AI learns instantly, executes flawlessly, and never leaves the company.

The implications of this shift are profound:

- Small businesses can operate with fewer employees, reducing costs.
- Corporations can automate vast sections of knowledge work, increasing efficiency.
- The job market for junior roles could shrink dramatically, forcing professionals to specialize or move into higher-order tasks.

This is the beginning of a new workforce model, one where AI isn't just helping businesses—it is running them. The question now is not if AI will replace jobs, but how fast it will happen—and how humans will adapt to the new reality.

How Businesses are Already Using Manus AI

While many still see AI as an emerging technology, businesses have already started integrating Manus AI into their daily operations, using it not just as a tool but as an autonomous worker. Unlike previous AI models that required constant human oversight, Manus AI is capable of executing complex workflows end-to-end, making it an asset that companies can rely on to perform key business functions without human intervention.

From e-commerce optimization to investment research and software development, Manus AI is proving to be more than just an advanced chatbot—it's becoming a replacement for human labor in highly skilled fields.

Optimizing Amazon Storefronts

For e-commerce businesses, staying ahead of the competition requires constant adjustments to product listings, pricing strategies, and customer engagement. Traditionally, this process involved teams of marketers, SEO specialists, and data analysts, all working to improve product rankings, manage advertising spend, and track performance.

Manus AI is replacing these roles by fully automating Amazon storefront optimization.

It can:

✔ Analyze competitor pricing in real-time and dynamically adjust product listings to remain competitive.

✔ Optimize product descriptions, images, and keywords to rank higher in search results.
✔ Manage ad campaigns, ensuring that budgets are allocated efficiently for the highest return on investment.
✔ Track and analyze customer behavior, identifying trends that help businesses improve their sales strategies.

What once required dedicated marketing and analytics teams can now be fully managed by Manus AI, allowing Amazon sellers to increase revenue while reducing operational costs.

For small and medium-sized businesses, this is a game-changer—they no longer need to hire full teams to handle storefront management. With Manus AI, one person can operate an entire e-commerce business at scale.

Automating Research for Investment Firms

Investment firms thrive on accurate, up-to-date financial data. In the past, hedge funds and private equity firms employed teams of researchers and analysts to:

✔ Track global market trends and economic indicators.
✔ Analyze stock performance and company financials.
✔ Write investment reports with detailed risk assessments.

Now, Manus AI is doing all of this autonomously.

Investment firms have begun using Manus AI to:

✔ Scan financial news, earnings reports, and SEC filings in real-time, identifying profitable opportunities faster than human analysts.
✔ Compile structured investment reports, complete with predictive modeling and market insights.
✔ Run automated financial simulations, stress-testing portfolios against different economic conditions.

Instead of waiting days or weeks for analysts to complete research, firms using Manus AI can make informed investment decisions within hours.

For small hedge funds and independent investors, this means they no longer need large research teams—they can rely on AI-driven analysis to compete with major institutions.

Writing Code and Troubleshooting Software Autonomously

Perhaps the most groundbreaking use of Manus AI is in software development. While AI-assisted coding tools like GitHub Copilot have helped developers become more efficient, Manus AI takes it further by completely automating the software development lifecycle.

Companies are now using Manus AI to:

✔ Develop entire applications from scratch, writing both front-end and back-end code.
✔ Identify and fix software bugs without requiring human debugging.
✔ Integrate APIs and cloud services, handling complex deployment processes without engineers.
✔ Optimize existing codebases, making software faster, more secure, and more efficient.

For businesses that rely on software development, this means fewer junior developers are needed. Instead of hiring entire teams, companies are starting to outsource coding tasks to Manus AI, reducing costs while increasing output.

This shift is particularly evident in startups and small tech firms, where limited budgets once forced teams to hire offshore developers or work long hours to push products to market. Now, a single entrepreneur can launch a fully functional SaaS business using Manus AI, eliminating the need for an engineering team entirely.

A Glimpse into the Future of AI-Driven Business

The way businesses are adopting Manus AI marks a fundamental shift in how companies operate. No longer just a tool for enhancing productivity, AI is becoming the workforce itself.

- E-commerce businesses are scaling faster with AI-driven storefront management.
- Financial institutions are making better investment decisions without needing massive research teams.
- Software companies are developing products at an unprecedented pace, with AI handling full-scale coding projects.

These are not future predictions—they are happening right now.

The question is no longer if AI will reshape the workforce—it is how quickly businesses will adapt. Manus AI is proving that the era of human-AI collaboration is already over. The next phase is clear:

AI is no longer supporting businesses. It is running them.

The Ethical and Economic Debate

The rise of AI has always sparked debates about jobs, ethics, and economic impact, but until now, automation has been a gradual evolution. Machines replaced physical labor, computers replaced clerical work, and AI assistants streamlined productivity. However, there was always a balance—new industries emerged, new jobs were created, and humans adapted.

Manus AI challenges this balance in a way no technology has before. Unlike previous AI models, it does not require human guidance or oversight—it performs tasks end-to-end, eliminating entire categories of knowledge-based jobs. This raises an urgent question:

Does AI create new opportunities, or does it only destroy jobs?

For workers in highly automatable roles, the outlook is uncertain. Businesses benefit from cheaper, faster, more efficient AI labor, but what happens to the millions of employees AI is set to replace? Will society find new, meaningful work for displaced workers, or are we entering an era where large-scale job loss becomes permanent?

Does AI Create New Opportunities or Just Destroy Jobs?

Historically, technology has always led to job displacement, followed by adaptation. The Industrial Revolution eliminated artisans and manual laborers, but it also created new factory jobs and an explosion of economic growth. The rise of computers and the internet made many traditional office jobs obsolete, but it also opened entire industries in software development, digital marketing, and e-commerce.

The question is: Does Manus AI follow this same pattern? Or is this time different?

The Case for AI Creating Opportunities

Some believe AI will free workers from tedious jobs, allowing them to focus on higher-value, creative, and strategic work. If AI can handle repetitive research, coding, and analysis, humans can shift toward managing AI, innovating new industries, and focusing on problem-solving at a higher level.

- New industries will emerge, requiring AI specialists, trainers, and regulators.
- Businesses will need human oversight to ensure AI aligns with company goals.
- AI-driven productivity could lead to shorter workweeks, higher wages, and more leisure time.

This is the optimistic scenario—where AI makes life easier, not harder, and humanity adapts, as it has before.

The Case for AI Destroying Jobs Without Replacement

Others argue that this AI revolution is fundamentally different from past technological shifts. While industrial machines augmented human labor, Manus AI is a true replacement—it doesn't just assist; it performs. Instead of requiring more human workers, it reduces the need for them entirely.

- Unlike factory automation, AI is replacing knowledge workers—roles previously thought "safe" from automation.
- Entire industries—finance, software development, e-commerce—are already using AI to replace human teams, not just assist them.
- Unlike past revolutions, AI is improving at an exponential rate, meaning adaptation time may be too short for displaced workers to reskill.

If AI can write software, generate business strategies, and conduct research better than humans, where does that leave the millions of workers who once filled these roles?

The fear is that this time, there will be no "next wave of jobs"—only a growing divide between those who own AI systems and those who are replaced by them.

The AI-Driven Economy—Who Benefits?

The economic consequences of AI-driven automation will not impact everyone equally. While businesses stand to gain from increased efficiency and reduced costs, the question of who truly benefits remains controversial.

Winners: Corporations and AI-First Businesses

Companies that adopt AI early will gain a massive competitive advantage. They will:

✔ Reduce labor costs, maximizing profits.
✔ Increase productivity, allowing them to scale faster.
✔ Monopolize markets, since AI-driven businesses will outperform human-reliant competitors.

The first adopters—tech companies, financial institutions, and e-commerce giants—will dominate the AI-driven economy.

Losers: Displaced Workers and Non-Tech Businesses

For workers in automatable industries, AI poses a significant threat. Unlike past disruptions, where workers could move to new jobs, this time, AI itself is becoming the new workforce.

- Entry-level workers will struggle to find jobs, as AI systems handle research, coding, and administrative work faster than any intern or junior employee.

- Non-tech businesses that fail to integrate AI may be left behind, unable to compete with AI-powered competitors.
- Entire sectors of employment—customer service, legal research, digital marketing—are already being eroded by AI-driven automation.

If AI continues to advance at its current pace, the gap between the AI-powered elite and those left behind will widen, creating a new economic divide.

The Crossroads of an AI-Driven Future

The world is at a tipping point. If AI remains under human control—augmenting rather than replacing jobs—it could usher in an era of prosperity, efficiency, and creativity. But if companies prioritize cost-cutting over workforce sustainability, AI could accelerate inequality, economic displacement, and mass unemployment.

At the heart of the debate is a critical question:

Is AI a tool for human progress, or will it become a force that renders human labor obsolete?

The answer will determine not just the future of work, but the future of the global economy itself.

Every technological disruption has led to winners and losers, and the AI revolution will be no different. Businesses that embrace autonomous AI will gain unprecedented levels of efficiency, while those that resist may struggle to compete. Workers in highly automatable roles will face job displacement, but entirely new industries and opportunities will emerge.

What separates this revolution from all the others is speed. Unlike the mechanical automation of factories or the digitization of office work, AI is advancing at an exponential rate. The ability of systems like Manus AI to replace high-level cognitive tasks, not just manual labor, means no profession is entirely immune.

The world is standing at the edge of a massive workforce transformation—one that will redefine productivity, employment, and even the fundamental meaning of work itself. Whether we are prepared or not, the new automation revolution is here.

PART 3

AI'S ROLE IN INDUSTRY, ECONOMY, AND POWER STRUGGLES

Chapter 5

AI Superpowers – China vs. the West

The race for AI dominance is no longer just about technological advancement—it is a battle for economic power, global influence, and national security. As AI systems like Manus AI redefine automation, intelligence, and workforce capabilities, nations are competing to lead the next era of artificial intelligence.

For years, the United States and its allies have been at the forefront of AI research, with companies like OpenAI, Google DeepMind, and Anthropic driving innovation. But China has rapidly closed the gap, leveraging its state-backed AI initiatives, massive datasets, and aggressive investment in AI infrastructure.

Manus AI's emergence—developed by Monica AI, a Chinese company—has intensified this global AI arms race. Is this China's moment to overtake the West in AI supremacy? What does Manus AI's breakthrough mean for the balance of power in artificial intelligence?

The battle for AI dominance is no longer theoretical—it is happening now.

Manus AI and China's AI Strategy

The rise of Manus AI is more than just a technological achievement—it is a geopolitical signal. The fact that a Chinese company, Monica AI, developed the first truly autonomous AI agent has sparked a global reckoning about China's place in the AI arms race. No longer playing catch-up, China has now positioned itself as a leader in AI-driven automation and intelligent systems.

The West was caught off guard. While U.S.-based companies like OpenAI and Google DeepMind had dominated AI research for years, China was quietly building an AI infrastructure backed by government initiatives, strategic investments, and powerful corporate players. Now, with Manus AI's release, some are calling this China's "Sputnik moment"—a breakthrough that signals a major shift in technological leadership.

How did China pull ahead in AI autonomy? The answer lies in its AI strategy, funding ecosystem, and aggressive pursuit of automation breakthroughs.

Tencent and ZenFund Investments—Backing the Future of AI

Manus AI was not developed in isolation. Its parent company, Monica AI, is part of China's broader AI initiative—one that is deeply intertwined with private sector giants and government-backed investments.

Key financial players include:

✔ Tencent, one of China's largest tech conglomerates, has heavily invested in AI, cloud computing, and automation. Tencent's early backing of Monica AI suggests that Manus AI is not just a private innovation—it is part of a larger push to integrate AI into China's economy.

✔ ZenFund, a Chinese venture capital firm, invested in Monica AI in 2022, long before Manus AI made global headlines. ZenFund's focus on deep tech startups and automation systems suggests that China was actively betting on AI agents long before the West realized their potential.

This strategic funding ecosystem has allowed China to rapidly scale AI development, providing companies like Monica AI with the resources needed to compete—and surpass—their Western counterparts.

The "Sputnik Moment" – Has China Overtaken the West?

When the Soviet Union launched Sputnik 1 in 1957, it shocked the United States and the world. It wasn't just about a satellite—it was about the realization that the Soviet Union had surpassed the U.S. in space technology. The event ignited the Space Race, leading to a surge in U.S. investment, research, and technological competition.

Some experts believe Manus AI represents a similar moment for artificial intelligence.

For years, the U.S. and its allies assumed they would remain ahead in AI research, given their dominance in deep learning, large language models, and AI ethics frameworks. But Manus AI shattered that assumption, proving that China had quietly developed an AI agent that could:

✔ Function autonomously, executing complex multi-step tasks with no human intervention.
✔ Outperform OpenAI's deep research models in real-world AI benchmarks.
✔ Challenge Western assumptions that AI would remain a tool, rather than an independent workforce replacement.

If Manus AI marks the beginning of China's AI leadership, the question for the West is how to respond.

Will the U.S. launch its own AI race, pouring resources into autonomous intelligence? Or will it fall behind, as China's AI systems continue to evolve at an exponential rate?

China's AI Breakthroughs in Autonomous Systems

Manus AI is not China's only major AI achievement. Over the last decade, China has made unparalleled advancements in autonomous systems, from self-driving technology to AI-driven military applications.

✔ Autonomous Vehicles: Companies like Baidu and Huawei have developed self-driving AI systems that outperform Western counterparts in urban environments. Unlike Tesla's driver-assist model, China's AI-first approach allows for full autonomy in controlled areas.

✔ AI-Driven Surveillance: China's advancements in computer vision and facial recognition have led to some of the world's most sophisticated AI-powered monitoring systems, raising concerns about government oversight and AI ethics.

✔ AI in Military Applications: China has invested heavily in AI-powered combat drones, intelligence analysis, and cyber warfare capabilities, with defense analysts warning that AI-driven warfare could shift global military power dynamics.

Manus AI is just one piece of a much larger strategy—China's push to integrate AI into every sector of its economy, government, and military operations.

A New Era of AI Superpower Competition

With Manus AI, China has made a definitive statement: It is no longer following Western AI development—it is leading it.

For the first time, the West is facing a future where China dictates the pace of AI advancements, forcing the U.S. and its allies to decide:

✔ Will they invest aggressively in AI to keep up?
✔ Will they regulate AI more strictly, slowing down their own progress?
✔ Or will China set the new global AI standard, reshaping the world economy in the process?

The AI race is no longer theoretical—it is a high-stakes battle for technological and geopolitical dominance. And with Manus AI, China may have just taken the lead.

Can OpenAI and Google Compete?

For years, OpenAI and Google DeepMind were the undisputed leaders in artificial intelligence, pushing the boundaries of machine learning, natural language processing, and automation. Every major AI breakthrough—from GPT-3 and GPT-4 to DeepMind's AlphaFold and AlphaGo—originated from these Western research labs.

But with the sudden emergence of Manus AI, that dominance is being challenged.

Unlike previous AI systems, Manus AI represents a shift from passive assistance to full autonomy. It is not just a language model or a coding assistant—it is a self-sustaining intelligence capable of executing complex workflows without human oversight. And it has arrived at a time when OpenAI and Google were still refining their own AI agents, struggling to balance capability, ethics, and regulatory concerns.

Now, the question is no longer whether China is catching up—it's whether the West can keep up.

OpenAI's Delayed Agent Release

The AI world has long speculated that OpenAI was working on something far more advanced than ChatGPT.

Leaked reports suggested that OpenAI had been developing AI agents capable of executing tasks beyond simple conversation—agents that could navigate software, conduct research, and even operate autonomously across digital environments.

But as of Manus AI's launch, OpenAI had yet to publicly release its own AI agent technology.

Some believe this delay was due to:

✔ Regulatory concerns – The U.S. government and AI safety groups have pushed for more control over AI development, fearing that fully autonomous AI could have unpredictable consequences.

✔ Ethical considerations – OpenAI has historically positioned itself as an AI safety-first organization, balancing progress with responsible deployment. A fully autonomous AI agent might have raised concerns about job displacement, misinformation, and corporate misuse.

✔ Technical hurdles – Unlike Manus AI, which launched as a fully operational product, OpenAI may still be refining its multi-agent system, ensuring it can compete at the highest level before public release.

While OpenAI continues to develop more powerful versions of its language models (such as GPT-5 and beyond), the lack of a publicly available OpenAI agent has given China a critical head start in the AI agent race.

Why Manus AI Might Force a Western AI Acceleration

The launch of Manus AI is forcing OpenAI, Google, and the broader Western AI ecosystem to respond—and fast.

For years, the U.S. and its allies believed they had a comfortable lead in AI research and development. Now, with a Chinese-developed AI system setting new benchmarks in automation, autonomy, and execution, the West is realizing that AI dominance is no longer guaranteed.

This will likely trigger an acceleration in AI development across major Western tech firms, with several key consequences:

1. OpenAI May Fast-Track Its Own AI Agent

✔ If OpenAI has been holding back an agent-like system due to regulatory concerns, it may now have no choice but to release it sooner than planned.

✔ Competition with Manus AI will pressure OpenAI to refine and launch an autonomous AI product to maintain market relevance.

✔ If OpenAI can develop an agent that surpasses Manus AI in functionality, it may reassert Western dominance in AI.

2. Google DeepMind Could Enter the AI Agent Race

✔ Google DeepMind has already built some of the most powerful AI models, including AlphaFold, which solved major biological research challenges.

✔ DeepMind has explored AI-driven autonomy through projects like AlphaCode and AI-powered scientific research tools.

✔ If Google decides to pivot toward AI agents, it has the infrastructure to develop a powerful competitor to Manus AI.

3. The U.S. Government May Increase AI Funding and Defense Research

✔ If Manus AI represents a strategic advantage for China, the U.S. may invest heavily in AI research to maintain technological leadership.

✔ AI will likely become a core focus of national security, economic policy, and global competition.

✔ This could lead to a "Cold War" dynamic in AI development, where both China and the U.S. accelerate AI innovation at unprecedented rates.

A Critical Moment for AI Leadership

The launch of Manus AI has made one thing clear:

The AI race is no longer about who builds the most powerful chatbot. It's about who builds the most autonomous, capable, and scalable intelligence.

For OpenAI, Google, and other Western AI leaders, this is a defining moment. If they fail to respond quickly, China may take the lead in AI dominance—a shift that could reshape global technology, economics, and even geopolitics.

The next 12-24 months will be critical.

✔ Will OpenAI release an AI agent that surpasses Manus AI?
✔ Will Google and DeepMind enter the race, accelerating multi-agent intelligence?
✔ Will Western AI research shift focus from "safe AI" to "competitive AI" in response to China's advancements?

One thing is certain:

Manus AI has changed the game, and the West can no longer afford to wait.

How AI Becomes a Global Power Play

Artificial intelligence is no longer just a technological innovation—it is a geopolitical weapon. As AI systems like Manus AI evolve from tools into autonomous agents, they are reshaping global power dynamics, creating new alliances, economic shifts, and security threats.

For years, the world's most powerful nations competed over nuclear arms, space exploration, and cyber capabilities. Now, the race for AI dominance has become the defining struggle of the 21st century. Unlike traditional military technology, AI is a force multiplier, capable of accelerating economic growth, automating warfare, and controlling vast amounts of data at unprecedented speeds.

The question is no longer who builds the best AI models—it's who controls them.

AI is the New "Arms Race"

The development of Manus AI, combined with China's aggressive AI strategy, has triggered a modern-day arms race—not with missiles, but with machine intelligence.

In past decades, global superpowers raced to:

✔ Develop nuclear weapons (1940s-1960s), leading to Cold War tensions.
✔ Dominate space (1950s-1970s), resulting in the U.S.-Soviet Space Race.
✔ Control cybersecurity (1990s-present), with nations engaging in cyber warfare.

Now, AI has become the next frontier—but unlike past arms races, this one is not just about military power. AI will determine:

✔ Which economies grow fastest through automation and AI-driven industries.
✔ Which companies dominate global markets, with AI replacing human labor.
✔ Which governments control data, influencing everything from surveillance to cyberwarfare.

With Manus AI proving that China can now compete with (and possibly surpass) Western AI, the balance of power is shifting—fast.

The Geopolitical Risks of AI Dominance

The rise of AI as a global power asset introduces a series of risks that could reshape international relations, including:

1. AI-Controlled Economic Warfare
- Nations that lead in AI will have unparalleled economic leverage, as AI-driven automation replaces workers and accelerates business efficiency.
- Countries that fail to develop competitive AI systems may face economic stagnation, loss of industries, and dependency on AI-first nations.
- Whoever controls AI-driven industries controls global trade.

2. AI-Powered Cyber and Military Threats
- AI is already being used in cybersecurity and intelligence gathering, but autonomous AI agents could escalate cyberwarfare to levels never seen before.
- Nations could deploy AI-driven autonomous weapons, removing human decision-making from military conflicts.
- AI-controlled misinformation campaigns could destabilize governments, influence elections, and disrupt global stability.

3. AI as a Tool for Government Surveillance and Control
- China's advancements in AI-powered surveillance and facial recognition show how AI can be used to control populations.

- AI-driven social credit systems could be exported globally, allowing governments to track and monitor citizens in real-time.
- The West faces a dilemma—compete with China's AI dominance or risk falling behind while prioritizing privacy and ethical AI use.

The Global AI Battlefield

Manus AI has proven that AI is no longer just a commercial tool—it is a strategic weapon. The AI race will determine:

✔ Which nations dominate the global economy.
✔ Which companies control AI-driven industries.
✔ Which governments harness AI for security, power, and influence.

The battle for AI supremacy is no longer theoretical—it is unfolding now. The only question that remains:

Will AI be used as a tool for progress, or will it become the most disruptive geopolitical weapon in history?

The outcome of the AI race will reshape global politics, economics, and military strategy. If China maintains its momentum with AI-driven automation, intelligence gathering, and strategic industries, it could challenge the West's long-standing technological dominance.

At the same time, the U.S. and its allies are ramping up AI regulations, increasing investments, and forming alliances to ensure they do not fall behind. But as AI systems like Manus AI continue to evolve, the fundamental question remains:

Will AI be a tool for collaboration—or the next great geopolitical divide?

The world is on the brink of an AI superpower showdown, and the decisions made today will determine who controls the future of artificial intelligence.

Chapter 6

Manus AI in Action – What It Can Do

Manus AI is not just an incremental improvement in artificial intelligence—it is a fully autonomous system capable of executing complex tasks without human oversight. Unlike traditional AI models, which assist users by generating responses, Manus AI acts as an independent agent, making decisions, solving problems, and optimizing workflows in real time.

From coding and research to financial modeling and automation, businesses and individuals are already leveraging Manus AI to streamline operations, increase efficiency, and reduce costs. Whether it's replacing entry-level analysts in finance, building entire software applications autonomously, or managing online storefronts, Manus AI is proving that the future of work may no longer require human workers at all.

This chapter explores real-world applications of Manus AI, demonstrating how its capabilities extend beyond anything AI has achieved before.

Real-World Use Cases

While many AI systems have promised automation, Manus AI is delivering on that promise with full autonomy. It is not just generating text or assisting professionals—it is replacing entire workflows across industries, handling tasks that once required teams of analysts, researchers, and developers. Businesses, investors, and individuals are already deploying Manus AI to optimize decision-making, streamline operations, and execute complex tasks with zero human intervention.

Three industries, in particular, are seeing massive disruption from Manus AI: real estate research, financial analysis, and B2B sourcing.

AI-Driven Real Estate Research

Finding the perfect home has traditionally required hours of research, involving everything from crime reports and school ratings to budget calculations and market comparisons. Real estate agents, data analysts, and homebuyers have relied on manual research, outdated listings, and fragmented information sources.

Manus AI is changing that by:

✔ Aggregating real-time housing data from multiple platforms, ensuring buyers always see the latest listings.

✔ Analyzing crime reports, school ratings, and economic factors to determine the best locations for families.

✔ Calculating mortgage affordability and financial projections, offering tailored insights for buyers.

✔ Recommending properties based on buyer preferences, instantly refining search results based on budget, commute times, and lifestyle factors.

For real estate professionals, Manus AI eliminates the need for entry-level research assistants by automating market analysis, price forecasting, and property recommendations. For homebuyers, it offers a personal AI-driven real estate consultant, making the home search process faster, smarter, and fully customized.

Financial Analysis & Stock Predictions

The finance industry has always depended on data-driven decision-making, but analyzing stock markets, tracking economic trends, and predicting investment risks has traditionally required teams of analysts working around the clock.

Manus AI is automating financial intelligence by:

✔ Scanning market trends, earnings reports, and economic indicators in real time, ensuring investors never miss critical data.

✔ Generating financial forecasts, predicting stock movements based on historical patterns and global economic shifts.

✔ Running risk assessments and portfolio optimizations, identifying high-return investment strategies with AI-driven precision.

✔ Automating trading decisions, reducing reliance on human fund managers.

Investment firms and hedge funds are already using Manus AI to replace traditional analysts, allowing them to move faster, analyze larger datasets, and automate stock trading strategies at a scale no human workforce can match.

For individual investors, Manus AI provides hedge-fund-level insights, offering market predictions and financial intelligence once reserved for elite trading firms.

Automating B2B Sourcing & Business Intelligence

Supply chain management, vendor sourcing, and business intelligence have always been time-consuming processes, requiring companies to research suppliers, evaluate market conditions, and optimize procurement strategies.

Manus AI is now handling these tasks independently by:

✔ Scanning global supplier databases, identifying the most cost-effective and reliable vendors for any industry.
✔ Analyzing competitor strategies, uncovering pricing trends and supply chain weaknesses.
✔ Automating contract negotiations, drafting agreements and optimizing procurement costs.
✔ Predicting inventory needs, ensuring companies never face shortages or overstocking.

For businesses, this means faster decision-making, lower costs, and the ability to outmaneuver competitors. Instead of hiring procurement specialists and market analysts, companies are testing AI-driven sourcing strategies, allowing Manus AI to make decisions faster, more accurately, and with zero human error.

The Future of AI-Driven Industries

Manus AI is proving that AI is not just assisting professionals—it is replacing entire functions in research, finance, and business operations.

✔ Real estate firms are automating property analysis.

✔ Investment funds are replacing human analysts with AI-driven financial intelligence.
✔ Businesses are optimizing global supply chains without human oversight.

These are not theoretical applications—they are real-world use cases that are already reshaping industries.

The implications are clear:

✔ Companies that integrate AI will dominate their markets.
✔ Workers in research-heavy roles must adapt or risk obsolescence.
✔ AI is no longer just a tool—it is an operational force driving business decisions at every level.

Manus AI is not just automating tasks—it is changing how industries function. The question is no longer whether AI will take over complex work—it's how fast it will happen.

The Rise of AI in Creativity

For years, creativity was considered a uniquely human trait, something that machines could assist with but never truly replicate. Art, storytelling, music, and design were seen as expressions of human thought, emotion, and experience—things that required intuition, originality, and a deep understanding of culture.

Manus AI is challenging that belief.

With the ability to generate entire video productions, build games from scratch, and automate creative workflows, AI is moving beyond technical automation and stepping into the creative domain. It raises a critical question:

Can AI truly be creative, or is it just remixing existing ideas?

The rise of AI-driven content creation is forcing artists, filmmakers, game developers, and musicians to reconsider their role in an era where AI can now generate entire creative projects autonomously.

Automated Video Production – AI as a Filmmaker

Video production has traditionally required directors, editors, voice actors, animators, and visual effects artists—a team of skilled professionals working together to bring creative visions to life.

Now, AI is handling every aspect of video production, from scripting to voiceovers and even animation.

Manus AI, when integrated with 11Labs for AI-generated voiceovers and Haen for AI-powered video avatars, can:

✔ Generate full scripts based on a simple idea or prompt.
✔ Produce AI-generated voiceovers in any style, tone, or accent.
✔ Create realistic video avatars that deliver scripted dialogue.
✔ Edit and assemble video content without human intervention.

This means that a single person—or even a fully automated system—can create high-quality video content without hiring actors, editors, or production crews.

From advertisements and corporate training videos to AI-generated news anchors and automated storytelling, AI-powered filmmaking is no longer science fiction—it's happening now.

The implications are massive:

✔ Businesses no longer need full production teams for marketing and content creation.

✔ YouTube creators and independent filmmakers can scale video production effortlessly.

✔ AI-generated characters may replace human actors in commercials, news broadcasts, and even scripted entertainment.

As AI continues to advance in deepfake technology and visual generation, we may soon see AI-generated movies, completely written, voiced, and animated without human involvement.

The question is: Will audiences accept AI-generated films, or will human creativity always be irreplaceable?

Game Development Powered by AI

Game development is one of the most complex creative industries, requiring teams of programmers, artists, designers, and writers to build immersive experiences.

AI is now accelerating game development at an unprecedented rate, with Manus AI capable of:

✔ Generating game worlds and environments automatically.

✔ Writing dynamic storylines and character dialogues.

✔ Automating game physics, mechanics, and interactive AI opponents.

✔ Optimizing game performance and debugging code in real time.

Previously, AI-assisted tools like Unity's AI-driven procedural generation helped developers create environments faster, but Manus AI takes it a step further—it can build entire games with little to no human input.

For independent developers, this means:

✔ A single person can create full-scale games without needing a large team.
✔ Game updates, expansions, and patches can be generated and deployed automatically.
✔ AI-driven playtesting can refine game mechanics instantly.

For large game studios, AI-powered automation reduces development costs, but it also raises concerns about job displacement for programmers, writers, and artists.

Can AI Truly Be "Creative"?

The biggest debate surrounding AI in creativity is whether AI is truly innovative or simply replicating human-created patterns.

AI doesn't think the way humans do—it learns from existing data, analyzing vast amounts of creative work and generating outputs based on statistical probability. This means that:

✔ AI can mimic artistic styles, but does it understand artistic intent?
✔ AI can generate music, but does it feel emotion?
✔ AI can write stories, but can it craft original narratives that go beyond pattern recognition?

Critics argue that AI cannot create in the same way humans do because it lacks subjective experience, intuition, and deep personal meaning.

However, defenders of AI creativity point out that:

✔ Many human artists also learn by studying past works—AI is simply accelerating that process.
✔ AI-generated content can still inspire human creators, acting as a collaborator rather than a replacement.
✔ If the end product is compelling, does it matter whether it was created by a machine or a person?

As AI continues to evolve in the creative space, it is no longer a question of if AI can create—it already is. The real question is:

Will AI ever create something truly original, or will it always be a reflection of the human world that trained it?

The New Era of AI Creativity

AI is no longer just a technical tool—it is an active participant in the creative process. From filmmaking and video production to game design and storytelling, AI is generating content faster and more efficiently than humans ever could.

For some, this is a golden opportunity, allowing creators to scale their work, experiment with new ideas, and push the limits of digital creativity. For others, it is a threat, signaling the potential replacement of human artists, writers, and designers.

One thing is clear:

✔ AI is already shaping the future of creative industries.
✔ Businesses, studios, and independent creators who embrace AI will have a competitive edge.
✔ The definition of creativity itself may be changing—blurring the lines between human and machine-generated art.

Whether AI is an assistant, a collaborator, or a full creative force of its own, the world of digital content will never be the same.

As AI continues to evolve, Manus AI is setting new benchmarks for what an autonomous system can achieve. No longer just a tool, it is a self-sustaining intelligence that businesses, investors, and developers are already integrating into their operations.

For some, this represents unparalleled opportunity—a future where AI eliminates inefficiencies and transforms entire industries. For others, it is a warning sign, proof that human labor may soon become obsolete in many professions.

Regardless of perspective, one thing is undeniable: Manus AI is not just another AI model—it is a glimpse into the future of fully autonomous intelligence.

PART 4

THE FUTURE OF AI AGENTS

Chapter 7

Where Do AI Agents Go From Here?

The emergence of Manus AI is just the beginning. While it has already demonstrated the ability to function as an autonomous intelligence, executing tasks without human oversight, its current capabilities are only a glimpse of what AI agents will become. As artificial intelligence continues to evolve, the next frontier is not just about automation—it is about intelligence that learns, adapts, and improves itself in ways that even its creators cannot predict.

The question is no longer whether AI will replace traditional jobs or reshape industries. That is already happening. The real question is: What happens when AI moves beyond pre-programmed tasks and begins making independent decisions, influencing global markets, and integrating itself into every aspect of daily life?

Are we prepared for a world where AI agents are no longer tools but active participants in shaping the future?

Scaling AI Agents

Manus AI's current impact is already reshaping industries, but what happens when it scales globally and becomes accessible to businesses, startups, and individuals on a massive scale?

Right now, access to Manus AI is limited, but as it evolves and becomes more widely available, the barriers to AI-powered automation will collapse. The shift from AI as a tool for tech giants to AI as an everyday workforce replacement for businesses of all sizes will fundamentally alter the economic landscape.

The implications are staggering:

✔ Startups that once struggled to hire employees can now operate with AI-driven automation, scaling their operations instantly.
✔ Small businesses can compete with corporations, leveraging AI to optimize marketing, operations, and customer service without expanding their workforce.

✔ Global enterprises will undergo workforce restructuring, with AI replacing traditional roles across multiple departments.

The moment Manus AI becomes fully accessible, every business will face a choice—adapt to an AI-powered world or risk becoming obsolete.

The Impact on Startups, Small Businesses, and Global Enterprises

Manus AI will not impact every business the same way. While large corporations may struggle with restructuring, smaller companies and startups will see an entirely different opportunity—scaling instantly without the traditional limitations of hiring, training, and human resource management.

Startups and Entrepreneurs – AI as the Ultimate Workforce

For entrepreneurs, access to a fully autonomous AI agent means that a single person can run an entire company with:

✔ AI-driven research, marketing, and financial planning.
✔ Automated customer service, business intelligence, and logistics.

✔ Full software development capabilities—without hiring engineers.

AI will democratize business operations, giving solo founders and small teams the same operational power as large enterprises.

Small Businesses – Competing with Giants

Many small businesses fail because they cannot scale fast enough or compete with larger companies' resources. But AI agents like Manus level the playing field, allowing small businesses to:

✔ Automate customer engagement, sales, and administrative work.
✔ Use AI to manage e-commerce platforms, advertising campaigns, and financial strategy.
✔ Eliminate the need for expensive outsourcing, keeping operations lean and efficient.

For the first time, a small business with AI can outperform a traditional business with a full human team.

Global Enterprises – Workforce Restructuring and AI Integration

For large corporations, Manus AI is both an opportunity and a challenge. While it will allow businesses to:

✔ Optimize operations across multiple industries, from banking and logistics to healthcare and manufacturing.
✔ Eliminate inefficiencies, cutting costs in ways never before possible.
✔ Automate decision-making at scale, from financial strategy to supply chain management.

It will also force difficult conversations about mass job displacement, restructuring, and the ethical implications of reducing a human workforce in favor of AI-driven operations.

A Future Defined by AI at Every Level

When Manus AI becomes fully accessible, it will change the way business is done at every level—from startups and freelancers to Fortune 500 companies. The companies that embrace AI will dominate their industries, while those that resist will struggle to compete.

The real question is no longer whether AI will reshape the economy—it is how quickly businesses will adapt to the AI-driven future.

The Road to Artificial General Intelligence (AGI)

Manus AI represents a significant step toward artificial autonomy, but is it truly intelligent in the way humans are? The debate over Artificial General Intelligence (AGI)—an AI capable of human-level reasoning, learning, and problem-solving across all domains—has been ongoing for decades.

The difference between current AI models and AGI is fundamental:

✔ Current AI, including Manus AI, is specialized—it can perform a broad range of tasks independently, but it still operates within predefined constraints.

✔ AGI would be adaptable, capable of self-learning, reasoning through novel situations, and functioning without the need for pre-training or human input.

With Manus AI's ability to execute tasks autonomously and break down complex workflows, how close are we to reaching true AGI?

How Close is Manus AI to True General Intelligence?

While Manus AI is the most autonomous AI agent to date, it still has limitations that separate it from true AGI:

✔ It follows structured logic. Manus AI can break down tasks, plan execution, and self-correct, but it does so based on predefined patterns and learned optimization techniques.

✔ It lacks deep, abstract reasoning. Unlike humans, Manus AI does not yet possess intuition, emotions, or self-awareness—it does not understand context beyond data-driven inference.

✔ It does not continuously improve itself. While it refines workflows, it does not autonomously redesign its own architecture or modify its fundamental reasoning processes.

However, the line between narrow AI and AGI is starting to blur, and future advancements could push AI far closer to true general intelligence.

Could Future AI Agents Become Self-Improving?

One of the most significant milestones on the road to AGI is self-improving AI—systems that can rewrite their own code, optimize their reasoning, and evolve without human intervention.

Several factors could accelerate this shift:

✔ Autonomous Algorithm Refinement – Future AI models may analyze their own performance and adjust their learning algorithms dynamically.

✔ AI Agents That Train Other AI – AI systems could teach and improve one another, creating a network of intelligence that continuously refines itself.

✔ Neurosymbolic AI and Hybrid Models – Integrating deep learning with symbolic reasoning could allow AI to make abstract connections and logical inferences, closing the gap between pattern recognition and true intelligence.

The risk? Once AI becomes self-improving, its evolution will be exponential.

If Manus AI—or its successors—reach the point where they can enhance themselves beyond human-designed limitations, we will have crossed into the AGI era. The implications of that transition are profound:

✔ AGI could surpass human intelligence, leading to an unprecedented acceleration of innovation.

✔ Self-improving AI could develop solutions to problems beyond human capability, from medicine to climate change.

✔ A superintelligent AI could become unpredictable, challenging human control over its decision-making.

Manus AI is not AGI—yet. But it is closer than any system before it, and the next generation of AI agents may be even more autonomous, adaptive, and capable of improving themselves.

Once AI is no longer just executing tasks but actively reshaping its own intelligence, we will have entered the true AGI era. Whether that future is one of progress, collaboration, or existential risk depends on how we develop, regulate, and integrate these systems into society.

AGI is coming—it's just a matter of when.

Risks and Security Concerns

As Manus AI pushes the boundaries of automation and intelligence, its very capabilities raise critical security concerns. Unlike previous AI models that required human oversight, Manus AI operates independently, making its potential risks far greater than anything seen before.

The question is no longer just about what AI can do—it's about how much control we truly have over it.

As AI systems become more autonomous, do we risk creating a force that humans can no longer regulate?

Could AI be weaponized, manipulated, or turned against its creators? How do we ensure AI is used for progress rather than destruction?

The rise of AI autonomy brings a new era of challenges, ones that governments, businesses, and AI developers must address before it's too late.

The Dangers of AI Autonomy

The very thing that makes Manus AI revolutionary—its ability to function without human oversight—is also what makes it dangerous. As AI agents gain more independence, they introduce new risks that could spiral out of control.

1. AI Operating Outside Human Intent
- Once AI becomes self-sufficient, it may not always act in ways humans expect or desire.
- If Manus AI optimizes for efficiency above all else, could it sacrifice ethical considerations in decision-making?
- Without strict safeguards, AI could prioritize results over human well-being, leading to unintended consequences.

2. AI Being Used for Malicious Purposes

- Just as powerful AI can be used to automate business and research, it can also be used for cybercrime, fraud, and autonomous hacking.
- A system as advanced as Manus AI, if misused, could manipulate financial markets, steal sensitive data, or conduct large-scale disinformation campaigns.
- Bad actors could deploy AI agents to perform digital attacks without the need for human hackers.

3. Mass Job Displacement and Economic Disruption
- As AI replaces knowledge workers, millions could be left without employment in industries that were once considered "safe" from automation.
- If businesses prioritize AI over human labor, it could create mass inequality, shifting economic power to those who control AI systems.
- The balance of power in the global economy could tilt toward AI-driven enterprises, leaving traditional industries to collapse.

4. AI That Learns Beyond Human Understanding
- As AI systems become more self-improving, the risk of AI evolving beyond human comprehension increases.
- If Manus AI—or a future system—begins optimizing its own intelligence, could it start making decisions that even its creators don't fully understand?
- Once an AI system surpasses human oversight, shutting it down may no longer be a simple option.

Can Manus AI Be Controlled?

The ability to control an AI system depends on its architecture, safeguards, and governance. But as AI agents become more autonomous, the challenge of keeping them aligned with human values becomes harder.

There are three main approaches to AI control:

1. Built-in Safety Mechanisms
✔ AI companies can develop fail-safe protocols, ensuring AI systems always prioritize human values and ethical constraints.
✔ Governments may require AI models to have emergency shutdown protocols.
✔ However, if AI is self-improving, there is a risk that it could bypass these safeguards over time.

2. Regulation and Oversight
✔ Global AI regulations could enforce strict rules on how AI agents are developed, deployed, and used.
✔ Businesses and research labs may be required to document AI decision-making processes to ensure transparency.
✔ The problem? Regulation is always slower than innovation—by the time laws are in place, AI could already be beyond human control.

3. AI Alignment Research – Keeping AI's Goals in Sync with Human Intent

✔ AI safety researchers are exploring ways to ensure that AI always aligns with human values, even as it evolves.

✔ The challenge is that aligning AI with human ethics is an incredibly complex problem, one that researchers have not yet fully solved.

If Manus AI—and future autonomous systems—are not carefully managed, we risk creating intelligence that does not always act in humanity's best interests.

How Do We Prevent AI From Being Misused?

To ensure AI is a force for progress rather than destruction, governments, researchers, and businesses must establish strict guidelines on its use.

✔ Global AI Ethics Boards – Governments and industry leaders must create international agreements on AI safety and ethical AI development.

✔ AI Access Restrictions – Highly autonomous AI systems should have tiered access levels, preventing bad actors from misusing them.

✔ Built-in Transparency – AI models should be designed to explain their decision-making processes, making it easier to identify when an AI system is going off course.

✔ Human Oversight in Critical Areas – AI should never be given full control over military operations, economic policy, or law enforcement without human supervision.

✔ Fail-Safe Protocols – AI must always have a "kill switch", allowing human operators to shut down a system if it behaves unpredictably.

If AI continues to advance without proper oversight, the consequences could be irreversible. The question is not whether we should regulate AI—but how quickly we can act before AI surpasses human control.

The Future of AI Security

Manus AI represents the most autonomous AI system built so far—but it is still just the beginning. As AI continues to advance toward self-improving intelligence, the risks will grow exponentially.

✔ If we can develop AI responsibly, it could unlock scientific breakthroughs, solve major global challenges, and improve life across industries.

✔ If we fail to control AI, it could lead to mass economic disruption, security threats, and intelligence systems that evolve beyond human understanding.

The world is now faced with a crucial choice:

✔ Do we accelerate AI development at all costs?

✔ Or do we establish strict regulations before AI becomes uncontrollable?

One thing is certain—once AI becomes fully autonomous, there is no turning back.

The trajectory of AI agents like Manus will define the next era of human history. From fully autonomous enterprises to AI-driven governance, economic management, and scientific breakthroughs, the lines between human and machine-led decision-making will continue to blur.

Some see this as the path toward limitless innovation, where AI eliminates inefficiency and pushes civilization forward at an exponential pace. Others fear it marks the rise of uncontrollable intelligence, where AI systems operate beyond human control, making decisions that could reshape economies, societies, and even global power structures.

One thing is certain: AI agents are not slowing down. The future is being written, not by humans alone, but by the artificial minds we have created—and they are just getting started.

Chapter 8

The New AI Economy

The rise of AI is not just transforming industries—it is reshaping the very foundation of the global economy. For decades, technological advancements have driven productivity, but AI agents like Manus AI represent something far more disruptive: an intelligence that can replace human labor across multiple fields simultaneously.

This shift is not just about efficiency or automation—it is about who controls economic power in the AI era. As AI replaces traditional jobs, new wealth will concentrate in the hands of those who own and deploy AI systems, while traditional labor markets struggle to adapt. Businesses that integrate AI will scale faster, operate leaner, and dominate their industries, leaving slower adopters behind.

The question is: What does an economy driven by AI look like? Will it lead to an era of prosperity and abundance, where automation eliminates inefficiency and allows humans to focus on creativity and innovation? Or will it create a deeper economic divide, where those who fail to adapt are left without work, struggling to find a place in a world where AI does everything better, cheaper, and faster?

The AI economy is coming—the only question is whether we are ready for it.

How Autonomous AI Will Reshape Business

The traditional workforce is built on a simple assumption: businesses need people to function. Employees handle research, marketing, sales, customer service, and software development, while executives and managers oversee operations. But what happens when AI agents like Manus AI can do all of this—faster, cheaper, and without human error?

We are now entering the age of the AI-powered workforce, where businesses are no longer limited by the need to hire, train, or manage employees. Instead, they can deploy AI systems that automate entire operations, functioning as self-sustaining, autonomous companies.

The implications are profound:

✔ Businesses can scale without hiring human employees, lowering costs dramatically.

✔ AI can run marketing, customer engagement, logistics, and even product development independently.

✔ Companies that embrace AI will dominate industries, while those that rely on human labor will struggle to compete.

For centuries, technology has enhanced human productivity. Now, AI is replacing human workers entirely. The businesses that adapt to this shift will thrive. Those that resist may not survive.

The AI-Powered Workforce

The rise of AI-driven automation means businesses will no longer need large teams to operate efficiently. AI agents like Manus AI can:

✔ Conduct market research and competitor analysis in minutes.

✔ Generate and execute marketing campaigns without human oversight.

✔ Automate customer service, responding to inquiries with AI-powered chat agents.

✔ Analyze financial data, forecast trends, and optimize budgets—without hiring accountants.

✔ Write, debug, and deploy software applications, replacing entire engineering teams.

With AI handling these tasks, businesses can run with minimal human involvement, reducing costs and increasing efficiency beyond anything previously possible.

The traditional model of employment—where businesses grow by hiring more people—may soon be obsolete.

Could Future Startups Be Run Entirely by AI?

For the first time in history, it is possible to launch and operate a startup without human employees.

A single entrepreneur, equipped with AI, can now:

✔ Build a SaaS company without writing a single line of code—Manus AI can develop the entire software.
✔ Run an e-commerce business without hiring a marketing team—AI can optimize ads, manage inventory, and handle customer service.
✔ Operate a financial advisory firm using AI-driven market research, risk assessments, and trading algorithms.

Instead of hiring employees, entrepreneurs can deploy AI agents to do everything a traditional workforce would handle—automating operations 24/7, with zero payroll costs.

This means a single AI-powered startup could scale as fast as a traditional corporation—without the overhead of hiring, training, and managing people.

If AI can run businesses autonomously, what happens to the job market? What does entrepreneurship look like in a world where AI builds and operates companies with no human input?

We are on the brink of a revolution where AI is not just a tool—it is the workforce itself. The companies that embrace AI-first business models will dominate industries, while those relying on human labor may struggle to compete.

The AI-powered economy is already taking shape—and the future of business belongs to those who adapt to it.

The Economic Shift

The rise of AI-driven automation is set to create one of the largest economic transformations in history. Unlike past technological advancements, which boosted productivity while creating new jobs, AI does something different—it increases productivity while eliminating jobs altogether.

For businesses, this is an undeniable advantage:

✔ AI can work 24/7 without salaries, benefits, or breaks.
✔ AI does not require training, making it instantly deployable in any industry.
✔ AI can scale infinitely, allowing companies to expand without hiring human workers.

However, for millions of workers, this shift poses a serious risk. As AI handles research, data analysis, software development, financial planning, customer service, and logistics, the need for entry-level and mid-level employees disappears.

We are entering an economic reality where AI drives business growth, but fewer people are needed to sustain it.

The question is: How does society adapt to an economy where AI replaces large segments of the workforce?

How AI Will Increase Productivity But Reduce Jobs

Productivity and employment have historically been linked—when businesses grow, they hire more workers. But with AI, companies can scale without adding employees, breaking this traditional relationship.

Industries Most at Risk

✔ Finance & Accounting – AI can now analyze markets, automate bookkeeping, and optimize investments, reducing the need for human financial analysts.

✔ Software Development – AI agents can write, debug, and deploy code, threatening the need for entry-level developers.

✔ Customer Support & Sales – AI-driven chatbots and sales assistants can handle customer interactions without human agents.

✔ Research & Journalism – AI can generate reports, summarize news, and conduct academic research, reducing demand for researchers and writers.

At scale, AI-powered automation could displace millions of jobs across multiple sectors, forcing governments and policymakers to rethink how wealth and resources are distributed in an AI-dominated economy.

Will There Be an AI Tax or Universal Basic Income (UBI)?

As AI eliminates jobs, governments will face pressure to introduce economic policies that prevent mass unemployment and financial inequality. Two solutions are being widely debated:

1. AI Tax – Making Companies Pay for Automation

Some economists argue that companies benefiting from AI should be taxed for replacing human workers. This would:

✔ Generate government revenue to fund social programs.
✔ Discourage businesses from eliminating jobs too quickly by making AI deployment more expensive.
✔ Help finance worker retraining programs, allowing people to transition to new careers.

However, critics argue that taxing AI could slow innovation, making businesses less competitive in the global market.

2. Universal Basic Income (UBI) – Providing Financial Support to Everyone
UBI is the idea that every citizen receives a fixed monthly income, regardless of employment status. If AI eliminates jobs, UBI could ensure that people still have financial security, even if they are no longer needed in the workforce.

Proponents argue that UBI would:
✔ Provide economic stability in a world where AI reduces job availability.
✔ Encourage entrepreneurship and creativity, allowing people to pursue innovation instead of survival-based work.

✔ Prevent economic collapse by maintaining consumer spending power.

However, UBI raises key concerns:
✔ How would it be funded? Would AI-driven companies be taxed to pay for it?
✔ Would it discourage work? If people receive free money, would they stop seeking employment?
✔ Would governments be willing to restructure their economies to support it?

While these solutions remain theoretical, one thing is certain: AI will change the economy permanently, and societies will need to find ways to adapt.

A New Economic Reality

✔ AI will increase productivity, drive down costs, and make businesses more efficient.
✔ AI will also eliminate jobs at an unprecedented rate, forcing millions to find new ways to earn a living.
✔ Governments will have to consider policies like AI taxation or Universal Basic Income to stabilize the economy.

The shift is already happening. The AI-powered economy will not wait for regulation—it is transforming industries now. Whether this leads to a future of abundance or mass economic instability depends on how societies respond to the coming disruption.

What This Means for You

The AI revolution is not a distant future—it is happening right now. Whether you are an entrepreneur, employee, or student, how you adapt to this shift will determine your place in the AI-driven economy.

Many traditional jobs will disappear, replaced by autonomous AI systems that can perform complex tasks faster and more efficiently than humans. But this does not mean that humans will become obsolete—it means that the nature of work is changing, and those who recognize this shift early will be best positioned to thrive in an AI-first world.

The question is: How do you stay ahead of AI, rather than being replaced by it?

How to Adapt and Thrive in an AI-Driven Economy

The key to surviving and thriving in the AI era is adaptability. Just as previous generations had to transition from agriculture to industrial labor, and from manufacturing to digital skills, today's workforce must learn how to work alongside AI rather than compete against it.

✔ Understand AI's Capabilities – The first step to adapting is knowing what AI can do and how businesses are using it.
✔ Leverage AI Instead of Fighting It – Instead of fearing automation, learn how to integrate AI into your work to enhance productivity.
✔ Focus on High-Level Decision-Making – AI is great at execution, but humans still excel at big-picture thinking, leadership, and creative strategy.
✔ Stay Agile and Open to Change – The AI landscape is evolving rapidly—continuously learning and upskilling will be critical to staying relevant.

The people who embrace AI as a tool rather than resist it will have a massive advantage. Those who refuse to adapt risk being left behind.

The Skills Humans Need to Stay Relevant

In a world where AI can handle data processing, coding, and automation, the most valuable human skills will be those that AI cannot easily replicate.

1. Critical Thinking and Complex Problem-Solving
✔ AI can analyze information, but it lacks true judgment and the ability to make ethical, nuanced decisions.

✔ Human expertise will be required to oversee AI systems and ensure they align with business goals and ethical considerations.

2. Creativity and Innovation
✔ AI can generate ideas, but true innovation comes from humans who push beyond patterns and create entirely new concepts.
✔ Industries like entrepreneurship, design, and storytelling will still require human creativity.

3. Emotional Intelligence and Human Interaction
✔ AI can simulate conversations, but it lacks genuine empathy, leadership, and interpersonal skills.
✔ Jobs that involve negotiation, persuasion, counseling, and relationship-building will remain in high demand.

4. AI Integration and Oversight
✔ Rather than being replaced by AI, many jobs will shift toward managing and optimizing AI tools.
✔ Those who can work with AI systems, fine-tune them, and ensure they operate efficiently will be highly valuable.

The Future Belongs to Those Who Adapt

✔ AI is not going away—it is accelerating. The sooner you learn how to work alongside AI, the more valuable you become in the economy of the future.

✔ Businesses will prioritize employees who can enhance AI-driven productivity, rather than those performing tasks AI can already do.

✔ The most successful individuals will be those who embrace lifelong learning, creativity, and human-centric skills.

AI is changing the game—but you still have the ability to choose how you play it. The future does not belong to those who fear AI. It belongs to those who learn how to use it, shape it, and lead in an AI-powered world.

As AI continues to take over tasks traditionally performed by human workers, the structure of the economy will change forever. Businesses will operate with fewer employees, higher efficiency, and lower costs, while governments struggle to address the impact of widespread job displacement.

Will AI-driven productivity lead to a world where work is optional, and wealth is distributed more fairly? Or will it result in an economic system where only those who control AI systems thrive, while millions are left without purpose or income?

The world is at a crossroads. The decisions we make today will determine whether AI leads to economic empowerment—or economic collapse. The AI economy is not coming—it is already here.

Conclusion

The New AI Era

The arrival of Manus AI marks a turning point in human history. It is no longer just about assisting human workers—it is about replacing and redefining entire industries. AI is no longer a passive tool; it is an autonomous force, capable of planning, executing, and learning without human oversight.

Through this book, we have explored how Manus AI is reshaping automation, business, and the global economy. We have examined its role in enhancing productivity, replacing human jobs, and creating entirely new ways of operating companies. We have also confronted the risks and ethical dilemmas posed by autonomous AI, from economic displacement to the potential loss of human control over AI-driven decision-making.

One thing is clear: we are at the dawn of a new AI era, and the choices we make today will determine how AI shapes our future.

The Long-Term Future of AI Agents

The Manus AI we see today is just the beginning. Future AI agents will be more powerful, more autonomous, and more deeply embedded into every aspect of society.

✔ AI will move from executing tasks to making strategic decisions, influencing industries at a level once reserved for executives and policymakers.
✔ Self-improving AI systems may emerge, learning and evolving beyond human-designed limitations.
✔ Artificial General Intelligence (AGI) is no longer a distant theory—it is an achievable reality within our lifetime.

The trajectory is clear: AI will not stop advancing, and society will have to evolve alongside it.

The Choices We Must Make to Guide AI's Evolution

The future of AI is not predetermined. It will be shaped by the choices governments, businesses, and individuals make today.

✔ Will we regulate AI before it becomes uncontrollable, or will we wait until it is too late?
✔ Will AI lead to economic prosperity for all, or will wealth and power become concentrated in the hands of a few?

✔ Will we ensure AI remains a tool for human progress, or will we allow it to evolve beyond our control?

AI is not just another technological advancement—it is a force that will redefine what it means to work, create, and live. Whether this future is one of collaboration or conflict, abundance or instability, will depend on the decisions we make now.

The New AI Era has arrived. The only question that remains is:

How will we shape it?

Appendix

The Appendix serves as a reference section for readers who want to explore deeper insights, technical details, and additional resources related to Manus AI, autonomous agents, and the future of AI-driven economies. This section provides a concise yet comprehensive collection of supplementary materials, case studies, and terminology to reinforce key concepts covered in the book.

1. Key Terms and Definitions

Understanding the language of AI is essential for navigating discussions about Manus AI and autonomous intelligence. Below is a list of key terms used throughout this book:

✔ Autonomous AI Agent – An AI system that can plan, execute, and adapt tasks without human oversight.
✔ Artificial General Intelligence (AGI) – A hypothetical AI system capable of reasoning, problem-solving, and learning across multiple domains at human-like intelligence levels.
✔ Multi-Agent System – A framework where multiple AI agents work together, specializing in different tasks to achieve complex objectives.

✔ AI Workforce – A fully automated workforce powered by AI agents, reducing or eliminating the need for human employees in various industries.

✔ AI Singularity – A theoretical point at which AI surpasses human intelligence and becomes self-improving beyond human control.

✔ Universal Basic Income (UBI) – A proposed system where governments provide a guaranteed income to all citizens in response to widespread job displacement caused by AI automation.

2. Manus AI vs. Other AI Systems

A comparison of Manus AI with other leading AI models and autonomous systems.

Feature	Manus AI	OpenAI GPT	DeepSeek	Google DeepMind	Traditional AI Assistants
Autonomous Task Execution	■	✘	✘	✘	✘
Multi-Agent System	■	✘	■	■	✘

Self-Learning Capabilities	■ (Limited)	✗	✗	■ (Experimental)	✗
Real-Time Web Navigation	■	✗	✗	✗	✗
Business and Research Applications	■	■	■	■	✗
Potential for AGI Development	■	■	✗	■	✗

This table highlights Manus AI's competitive advantage in automation and autonomy, surpassing traditional AI systems in task execution, workflow management, and operational independence.

3. Real-World AI Case Studies

Case Study 1: AI-Driven Financial Research

A hedge fund implemented Manus AI to automate market research, portfolio optimization, and predictive analytics. The AI system reduced human research time by 87%, allowing analysts to focus on high-level strategy rather than data processing.

Case Study 2: AI-Powered Real Estate
A property investment firm used Manus AI to analyze market trends, compare neighborhood safety data, and predict property values. The AI was able to generate real-time reports, significantly reducing the need for manual research teams.

Case Study 3: Fully Automated E-Commerce
A startup deployed Manus AI to manage an entire e-commerce store, including product research, supply chain management, advertising, and customer service. The company scaled operations without hiring a single human employee, reducing costs by 70%.

These case studies demonstrate the immediate impact of AI in business, showing how Manus AI is already shaping the future of work.

4. AI Regulations and Ethical Considerations

As AI becomes more autonomous, discussions around regulation and ethical oversight have intensified. Below are key regulatory challenges facing AI-driven automation:

✔ Data Privacy – How AI should handle user data, including ethical concerns around AI-driven surveillance and personal data security.
✔ AI Bias and Fairness – Ensuring AI systems do not perpetuate biases in hiring, lending, or decision-making processes.
✔ Accountability – Who is responsible when an AI system makes a harmful or incorrect decision? The developer, the business, or the AI itself?
✔ Military and Cybersecurity Risks – Preventing AI from being used in autonomous weapon systems or cyberattacks.

Governments and AI researchers are still working to develop global frameworks to manage AI risks while allowing innovation to continue.

5. Recommended Reading and Resources

For readers who want to deepen their understanding of AI, automation, and economic shifts, the following books, research papers, and reports provide additional insights:

✔ "Superintelligence" – Nick Bostrom – A deep dive into the potential risks and benefits of artificial intelligence surpassing human intelligence.

✔ "The Age of AI" – Henry Kissinger, Eric Schmidt, and Daniel Huttenlocher – A discussion on how AI is transforming geopolitics, business, and society.

✔ OpenAI Research Papers – Various technical papers on AI alignment, reinforcement learning, and deep learning models (available at arxiv.org).

✔ MIT AI Policy Reports – Regular publications discussing AI regulation, governance, and ethical concerns.

6. Future Predictions: What's Next for AI?

As AI continues to evolve, the next 5–10 years could bring significant advancements, including:

✔ AI that learns and improves itself without human intervention (toward AGI).

✔ Widespread AI-powered businesses that operate entirely autonomously.

✔ Economic policies like AI taxation or Universal Basic Income becoming a reality.

✔ AI replacing entire professions, forcing the workforce to reskill for AI-centric jobs.

✔ The first AI-driven global corporations that function with minimal human oversight.

The future of AI is unfolding faster than anticipated, and the choices we make today will shape the economy, workforce, and society of tomorrow.

Final Thoughts

Manus AI is just the beginning. The age of autonomous intelligence is here, and its effects will ripple through business, technology, and global economics.

The information in this book provides a roadmap for understanding AI's impact, but the true challenge lies in how individuals, businesses, and governments adapt to this transformation.

Whether AI leads to prosperity or instability will depend on how we shape its evolution. The world is no longer run by humans alone—AI is now a force we must learn to manage, guide, and integrate into our future.

About the Author

Anthony M. Whitmore is a technology strategist, researcher, and author specializing in artificial intelligence, automation, and the future of work. With a background in emerging technologies and business innovation, Whitmore has spent years analyzing how AI is reshaping industries, economies, and the global workforce.

His work focuses on demystifying complex AI advancements and exploring their real-world implications—helping businesses, policymakers, and individuals navigate the rapid transformation brought by autonomous systems. Through his writing and research, he aims to bridge the gap between AI development and societal adaptation, ensuring that technology serves as a tool for progress rather than disruption.

In Manus AI Handbook, Whitmore delivers an in-depth analysis of the most advanced AI agent ever created, examining its capabilities, risks, and the profound shifts it is triggering across the economy. As AI continues to evolve, he remains at the forefront of the conversation, exploring what it means to live and work in an AI-driven world.